Fabulous
Woven Jewelry

Fabulous
Woven Jewelry

Plaiting,
Coiling,
Knotting,
Looping &
Twining
with
Fiber &
Metal

Mary Hettmansperger

LARK BOOKS

A Division of Sterling Publishing Co., Inc.
New York

EDITOR:
Katherine Duncan Aimone

ART DIRECTOR:
Dana Irwin

COVER DESIGNER:
Barbara Zaretsky

ASSISTANT EDITOR:
Rebecca Guthrie

ASSOCIATE EDITOR:
Nathalie Mornu

ASSISTANT ART DIRECTOR:
Lance Wille

ASSOCIATE ART DIRECTOR:
Shannon Yokeley

EDITORIAL ASSISTANCE:
Delores Gosnell

EDITORIAL INTERNS:
Kelly J. Johnson and David Squires

PHOTOGRAPHER:
Stewart O'Shields
(www.stewartoshields.com)

ILLUSTRATOR:
Mary Hettmansperger

Paintings shown in the background
on title page, table of contents
page, and pages 38, 50, 62, and
92 are by Steven Aimone

Library of Congress Cataloging-in-Publication Data

Hettmansperger, Mary.
  Fabulous woven jewelry : plaiting, coiling, knotting,
looping & twining with fiber & metal / Mary
Hettmansperger.
      p. cm.
  Includes index.
  ISBN 1-57990-614-1 (pbk.)
  1. Jewelry making. 2. Fiberwork. 3. Wire craft. 4. Braid.
  I. Title.
TT212.H46 2005
                                745.594'2--dc22

10 9 8 7 6 5 4 3

Published by Lark Books, A Division of
Sterling Publishing Co., Inc.
387 Park Avenue South, New York, N.Y. 10016

Text © 2005, Mary Hettmansperger
Photography © 2005, Lark Books
Illustrations © 2005, Lark Books

Distributed in Canada by Sterling Publishing,
c/o Canadian Manda Group, 165 Dufferin Street
Toronto, Ontario, Canada M6K 3H6

Distributed in the United Kingdom by GMC Distribution Services,
Castle Place, 166 High Street, Lewes, East Sussex, England BN7 1XU

Distributed in Australia by Capricorn Link (Australia) Pty Ltd.,
P.O. Box 704, Windsor, NSW 2756 Australia

If you have questions or comments about this book, please contact:
Lark Books, 67 Broadway, Asheville, NC 28801
(828) 253-0467

Manufactured in China

  ISBN 13: 978-1-57990-614-6
  ISBN 10: 1-57990-614-1

For information about custom editions, special sales, premium and corporate
  purchases, please contact Sterling Special Sales Department at 800-805-5489
    or specialsales@sterlingpub.com.

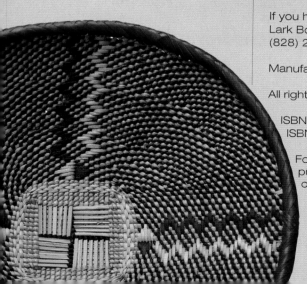

CONTENTS

INTRODUCTION

I FIND GREAT INSPIRATION IN NATURE, LIFE, AND CHANGE. IN THIS SPIRIT, I ENCOURAGE YOU TO LEARN THE TECHNIQUES AND CONCEPTS OF THIS BOOK AND USE THEM TO DEVELOP YOUR OWN WORK. TO GROW ARTISTICALLY YOU MUST TAKE CHANCES, GIVE YOURSELF TIME TO EXPLORE YOUR CREATIVE THOUGHTS, AND THEN MOVE FORWARD! MY MOST SUCCESSFUL IDEAS AND DESIGNS HAVE DEVELOPED FROM EXPERIMENTATION AND PLAY.

Mary Hettmansperger
Tea Cozy, **1999**
16 x 3 1/2 x 2 inches
Waxed linen; twined
PHOTO BY DAVID BAIRD

Mary Hettmansperger
Dark and Light of It, **2004**
2 1/2 x 5 inches
Waxed linen; twined
PHOTO BY DAVID BAIRD

A couple of decades ago in college, it suddenly dawned on me one night that I was on the wrong path. I had plans to become a nurse to satisfy my more sensible, practical side. However, I knew deep inside that to be happy and fulfilled I had to do something creative and artistic, even if it meant taking the risk of less job security.

My earliest memories include drawing and creating. My father had an immense amount of artistic ability, but he never had time to engage his talent to the fullest. So when my desire to pursue art took precedence over everything else, I gave it my full attention.

Several years later, after a move to Indiana, I married the man of my dreams, and we began a family. At Indiana University, I began my formal education in art, convinced that I was finally in the right place. I was immediately attracted to fiber arts, and everything I created had a textural and three-dimensional quality.

Eventually, I turned to something that had fascinated me since childhood—making baskets. Before long, I was selling functional baskets and teaching basket making. But I struggled with the lack of creative freedom in this kind of work, so I began to experiment with the vessel shape and natural materials. I relied on the foundational techniques of basketry that I had learned as the basis for the work.

While teaching at an art center in Nebraska, I was offered a gallery space in which to show my work. I had been making work that stretched the possibilities of rib basketry construction. This exhibition opportunity spurred me on, and I filled the gallery with unusual pieces. Eventually, I experimented with turning a small ribbed basket into a necklace pendant. I created more jewelry using basic basketry techniques, adding metal to my list of materials. The body of work grew.

My work with jewelry led to teaching others how to make fiber and metal jewelry. This work has become a major part of my career, and I lead workshops across the country, from art and craft schools to national conferences. It's a dream come true to draw on this experience to write a book about making innovative jewelry.

The book is divided into chapters headed with familiar basketry techniques: plaiting, twining, looping, knotting, and coiling. After you're introduced to materials, supplies, and tools, you can begin with any of the chapters that you wish. At the beginning of each chapter, you'll learn the basics of the technique through my easy-to-follow illustrations and text. As you make the projects, refer back to these sections.

Some projects are made with traditional materials, such as ash, while others are created with newer media such as metals or found objects. You'll also see interesting variations on the projects that will expand your thinking about design and materials.

Whether you currently make baskets or jewelry, you'll enjoy making these beautiful wearable pieces. As you try your hand at them, allow yourself time to explore the new ideas that will undoubtedly occur to you.

It's my hope that this book effectively shares things I've learned along the way, while giving you inspiration to discover your own creative path with fiber and metal jewelry.

Mary Hettmansperger
Twined Silver Pin, 2005
Silver wire, seed beads; twined
PHOTO BY STEWART O'SHIELDS

Mary Hettmansperger
Quiver-Shaped Necklace, 2005
Ash, linen, birch bark, beads; plaited and twined
PHOTO BY STEWART O'SHIELDS

MATERIALS AND SUPPLIES

FROM TRADITIONAL BASKETRY MATERIALS, SUCH AS
REED AND ASH, TO COLORFUL WAXED LINEN AND
EMBROIDERY THREAD, THE MATERIALS AND SUPPLIES
DESCRIBED IN THIS SECTION INTRODUCE YOU TO
MANY POSSIBILITIES FOR MAKING WOVEN JEWELRY.

You can weave with copper or silver wire to produce beautiful results. And many jewelry pieces incorporate natural materials such as seedpods or driftwood—even beach glass—as a part of their overall design and aesthetic.

This section serves as a handy reference as you work through the projects. Before you begin, thumb through it to get an idea of the creative things you'll be able to do with a range of materials and supplies.

TRADITIONAL WEAVING MATERIALS

Materials used for traditional basketry work are used to make small basket forms. Use narrow versions of reed, black ash, raffia, and birch bark. Pine needles are traditionally used for coiling.

■ REED

This natural material that comes in a variety of widths is commercially prepared for basketry. A narrow version works

Raffia, reed, and ash

well for small pieces—$^{11}/_{64}$ flat oval is the standard size used in the projects. You can also use $^{11}/_{64}$ flat–flat reed. Soak reed in water for five to 10 minutes, or until it's pliable.

■ BLACK ASH

Double-satin black ash, made from the black ash tree, is commercially prepared for basketry. It's my personal preference for woven jewelry because it's supple and ribbon-like, making it easy to weave. It has a nice smooth finish on both sides. The following widths are used in the projects: $^1/_8$, $^1/_{32}$, and $^1/_{16}$ inch.

Black ash is available through basketry suppliers. Some basket makers harvest and prepare their own material, but this process is very time consuming.

Because black ash shrinks after drying, you should not soak it. If it's too wet while you're weaving it, you'll end up with loose weaving containing holes or gaps. Instead, keep it damp and pliable while working with it by wetting your hands occasionally, running the ash over a dampened sponge, or spraying it lightly with water.

As a general rule, use the least amount of water that you can to keep it workable. When weaving an entire piece out of black ash, it's a good idea to stop and let it dry slightly as you work. After this, pack it down to tighten the weaving.

■ RAFFIA

Raffia, a tan material made from palms that has a paper-like quality, is a great binding material to use for coiling. It can also be added to looped or plaited pieces to lend them a nice texture. You can separate it into a variety of widths, even thread-thin, and it will still be very strong. It can be purchased through both basketry and craft suppliers. Dyed raffia is pretty, but if you use it to make jewelry, you run the risk of the color bleeding onto clothing.

■ BIRCH BARK

Correctly prepared birch bark weaves like ribbon. Thick sheets of it are harvested before being separated out into thinner layers. If it's thin enough, it won't crack when you weave it. You don't need to dampen it to make it pliable.

Birch bark ranges in color from light tan to deep reddish brown, depending on the time of harvest and the particular tree.

You can harvest it yourself, but it is a difficult process with many variables. Instead, purchase it through a basketry supplier.

■ PINE NEEDLES

Pine needles are wonderful to use as a core for coiled jewelry. I prefer the longer varieties because they go further. You can collect

Pine needles, birch bark, and wild cherry bark

pine needles yourself or buy them through basketry suppliers.

If you collect the needles yourself, look for fresh green ones on a trimmed branch or a tree that's recently fallen, since needles that have been on the ground for a while might be too brittle to use.

If you dry them in the sun prior to using them, they'll turn a nice brown color. Turn them over regularly during the course of about three weeks of drying. If you dry needles in the shade or inside, they'll retain a light, subtle, green tone. This process also takes about three weeks.

After they've dried completely, wash them off with a mild detergent to clean off any dirt and insects. Let them dry again in a well-ventilated area for about 24 hours before storing them, because if they aren't completely dry, they might grow mold. Then store them in anything from plastic bags to storage containers.

When used for coiling, the dried needles may need to be soaked before they're used. If a needle from the batch wrapped around your finger several times breaks or cracks, they need soaking.

Soak them about 30 minutes to an hour in warm to hot water. After soaking, wrap them in a towel and place them in a plastic bag to allow them to mellow overnight. If your work is interrupted, store mellowed pine needles in the freezer to avoid the soaking process again.

Since jewelry pieces are so small, you can make the whole coiled piece from wet needles. Keep them in the damp towel so they'll remain pliable throughout the process.

NON-TRADITIONAL WEAVING MATERIALS

Using traditional basketry techniques to weave non-traditional materials gives you a lot of creative latitude when you're making jewelry. You have access to almost any color if you use embroidery floss. Waxed linen is beautiful, substantial, and easy to weave. It is also used to make neck cords and chains. You can add unexpected texture and color to the work by weaving with various types of wire.

Waxed linen and embroidery thread

■ WAXED LINEN

Waxed linen is a strong, consistent material that works wonderfully for weaving small woven jewelry and making neck cords. It comes in a wide range of colors and various weights. In the projects, 3- and 4-ply are used for twining, looping, knotting, and binding. Irish waxed linen is the best you can buy, and I recommend that you use this variety for making the projects.It can be purchased from bead, basketry, and bookbinding suppliers. If you can't find it in a store, the Internet is a great place to shop for it.

■ EMBROIDERY FLOSS

Embroidery floss, with its beautiful sheen, is a wonderful material for weaving. It is usually sold in 7-yard packages. It's inexpensive and readily available in fabric, craft, knitting, and other stores. Because it comes in a wide range of shades, it's easy to create gradual color changes, adding depth and drama to your work.

WIRES

Using wire was at one time unconventional in the basketry world, but it has now grown in popularity. It is pliable as well as beautiful, making it a natural for woven jewelry.

The gauge of wire determines its size, and the smaller the number, the larger the size. Two sizes are used for the projects in this book: 24-gauge wire for weaving and stitching, and sturdier 18-gauge wire for making spokes and other structural portions of the jewelry.

You can finish the ends of larger-gauged wires used for spokes by forging them with a hammer and anvil (see page 27). You can also finish ends of wire that are copper, silver, or tin-coated by burning and rounding the ends with a torch (see page 28).

Copper, tin-coated, and brass wire can be purchased through metal or jewelry suppliers as well as home supply and hardware stores. Silver wire is found primarily through jewelry suppliers. Colored and craft wire is available in most craft supply stores.

■ COPPER WIRE

Copper wire is very pliable and is easy to weave. The larger version can be used for spokes. Buy bare wire that doesn't have a protective coating or tarnish inhibitor so that it will tarnish as it ages, lending it a rich patina that compliments the other materials.

■ SILVER WIRE

Silver wire is a beautiful material for jewelry-making that's worth the extra expense. If you're just beginning to work with wire in jewelry, you'll find it more difficult to weave than copper, since it's less flexible. Try mastering the techniques with copper, and then use silver.

■ TIN-COATED COPPER WIRE

A less expensive alternative to silver wire is tin-coated copper wire. Although not as shiny as silver, it is still very nice. With age, it will remain silver but become duller. It's aged look is compatible with found objects in jewelry.

■ BRASS AND COLORED WIRE

Both brass and colored craft wire are practical for weaving small jewelry projects. You should not use the torch with either of these wires, however.

Brass, copper, and colorful craft wires

COPPER SHEETING, MESH, AND FOIL

Copper is my favorite material to use in jewelry. In addition to its inherent beauty, it is relatively inexpensive and readily available. Sheeting, mesh, and wire are used in the projects for weaving, structural components, and embellishments.

It gains a patina as it ages, turning a darker and richer color. If you apply heat to it with a torch, colors will appear on the surface, ranging from yellows and pinks to dark purples, reds, and oranges (see page 31).

■ COPPER SHEETING

You can cut pieces of copper sheeting and drill it with holes before using it as a structural component for weaving. Eighteen-gauge sheeting is used in all of the projects because it is rigid but easy to cut. You can add a patina by applying heat to it, and you can deckle the edges by forging them (see page 27).

■ COPPER FOIL

Copper foil is a thin sheet metal that varies in thickness. It is extremely easy to use and manipulate. It can be cut with scissors or folded and bent with needle-nose pliers. For plaiting and weaving, my preference is a .002-width, which is quite thin. You can order copper foil through metal or jewelry suppliers, and some craft and hardware stores carry it as well.

■ COPPER MESH

Copper mesh is a form of woven wire cloth that adds nice texture to jewelry pieces. It comes in different sizes, and the fine grade of 100 x 100 mesh per inch works well because it is easy to manipulate and cut.

MOLDS

Many of the projects in this book are made on a mold, either temporary or permanent. A temporary mold is used to shape the piece while it's being woven, and then it's removed. Cardboard shapes work well as temporary molds.

Permanent molds, such as pretty glass or interesting bits of driftwood, are a visual component of the piece of jewelry and are not removed. Think outside of the box in this area: I've found that there are many unusual items that can be used for permanent molds.

Top: Copper sheeting, mesh, and foil

■ CARDBOARD FORMS

Simple cardboard forms, such as empty tissue or towel rolls, or yarn cones, work well as temporary molds for shaping woven pieces. The texture of the paper grips the weaving so that it doesn't slip. If needed, you can stick pins into the cardboard to anchor the materials as you weave.

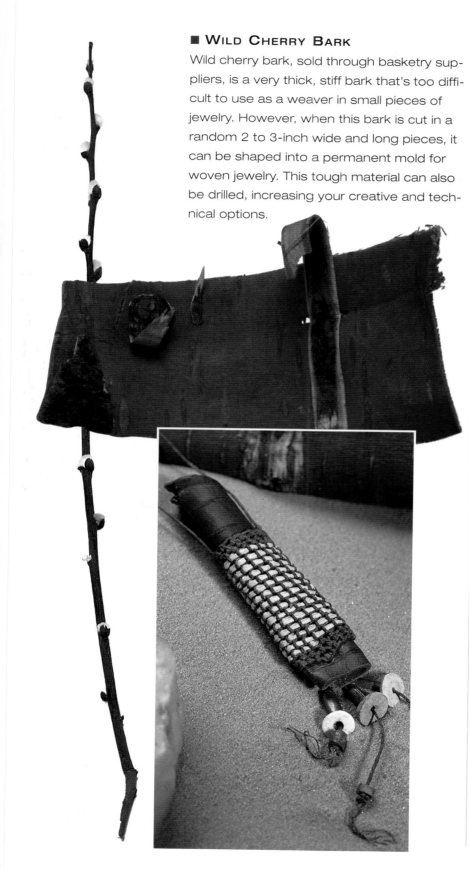

■ WILD CHERRY BARK

Wild cherry bark, sold through basketry suppliers, is a very thick, stiff bark that's too difficult to use as a weaver in small pieces of jewelry. However, when this bark is cut in a random 2 to 3-inch wide and long pieces, it can be shaped into a permanent mold for woven jewelry. This tough material can also be drilled, increasing your creative and technical options.

To make a mold from the bark, soak a flat piece of it in warm water for about an hour. Then shape or roll it into a shape of your choice, and clamp it with clothespins while it dries.

■ SEEDPODS AND WOOD

After a long walk in the woods, I always come back home with my pockets full of things I've collected to use in my jewelry. For instance, I love seedpods because of their unique shapes and textures. They make wonderful molds for looped or knotted jewelry. Choose pods that aren't too fragile. To prepare pods, spray them several times with a matte fixative to bring out the natural colors and keep them from deteriorating over time.

Small pieces of driftwood or other weathered wood also make interesting molds. Make sure that the wood you choose is strong, hard, and aged. It should be clean and free of insects. Wood, like pods, can be gathered almost anywhere. You can also find a wide selection of natural dried materials at basketry, floral, and craft suppliers.

To preserve the natural beauty of the wood, spray it with a matte spray fixative before you attach weaving to it. You can also treat the wood with wood finishes and stains, but make sure that these products don't rub off on clothing.

■ BEACH OR TUMBLED GLASS

If you can't go scavenging on the beach, beach or tumbled glass is readily available through most bead shops. These materials make beautiful permanent molds for jewelry.

■ ROCKS

Rocks, with all of their varied textures and coloration, also make interesting permanent molds. Look for smooth, rounded, rocks that will be complemented by surface weaving without needing alteration.

Driftwood and seedpods

Stone donuts, tumbled glass, and other molds

■ STONE DONUTS

These donuts are made from a variety of stones and are available in many sizes. Because they have holes, they work well as permanent molds, because you can attach the material to them easily. You can purchase them through bead shops or jewelry suppliers.

■ OVERSIZED GLASS BEADS

Oversized glass beads make nice permanent molds. Like donuts, you can anchor the weaving through the hole.

ADDITIONS AND EMBELLISHMENTS

This section introduces you to a few of your options for embellishing jewelry pieces, all of which are used in the projects. They're available through a variety of different types of stores—craft supply stores, beading suppliers, fabric stores, scrapbooking stores, hardware stores, flea markets, and antique stores—to name a few!

I've found that scrapbooking supplies are a great resource for jewelry. For instance, eyelets now come in a broad range of colors, and you can purchase mica in ready-to-use sheets.

■ MICA

Mica is a natural-occurring, amber-colored material that can be purchased at craft supply and scrapbooking stores. Because it is semi-translucent and textured, it contrasts nicely with copper jewelry components. In this book, it's used to create windows or layers in small metal books. You'll fasten it to the surface of metal by drilling holes in it before using eyelets or small nuts and bolts to secure it.

■ FOUND OBJECTS

Found objects add visual interest to your jewelry. Look through bins at a hardware store, and let your imagination roam. Antique coins, foreign coins, and bus tokens also make great additions to jewelry. By using them in jewelry, you remove them from their usual context.

Flattened bottle caps or metal can lids are easy to find and make an interesting addition to jewelry. I use all sorts of caps—whether they're old ones that I've found or new ones purchased from craft or scrapbooking stores.

Rusted caps give you a nice surface with which to work, but they need to be cleaned with soap, water, and a wire brush to loosen any rust particles from the surface. Always wear a dust mask to avoid inhaling small rust particles.

Mica, stones, beach glass, and bottle caps

Decorative papers, fabric, and eyelets

After they're dry, apply non-yellowing, matte fixative to the smoothed surface. After the cap dries, test the finish by rubbing it with a clean white cloth.

To use caps or lids, you'll usually drill holes in them. The edges are drilled before wire spokes are added. Caps fitted with rubber seals are easier to drill because the rubber helps hold the piece in place.

To drill the holes, put on safety glasses, and punch small holes with your awl and hammer before drilling. If you can clamp the cap in place while you're using the drill, it will be safer. When you do the drilling, protect your hands with heavy protective gloves, such as leather, while you hold the cap in place on your workbench.

■ EYELETS

Insert metal eyelets into holes drilled in metal, such as caps or pieces of metal sheeting. These small pieces of hardware are available in many colors and finishes at craft, scrapbooking, and fabric stores. An eyelet tool for mounting them comes with the eyelets. Always wear leather gloves to protect your hands when you're inserting eyelets into metal.

■ PAPER

Because scrapbooking has become so popular, papers in any size, texture, color, or design can be found at most craft supply stores. In the projects, paper pages are added to metal covers to form small books (see page 46). Collaged papers are also a

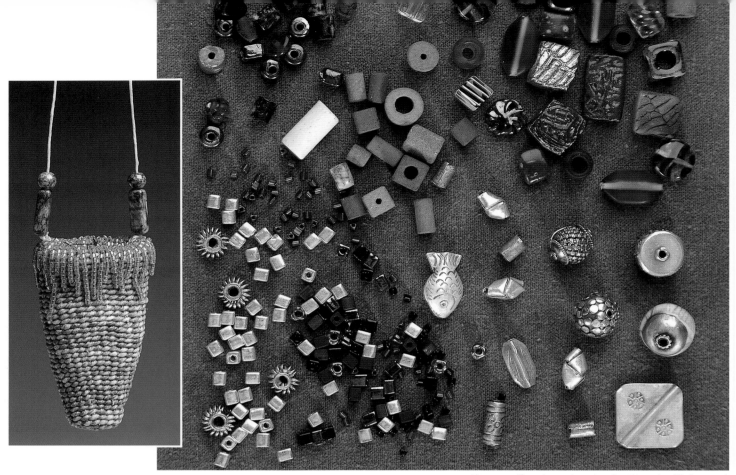

Decorative beads used as embellishment

nice addition to these small metal books. When you use paper for collage, adhere it with a non-yellowing matte medium or glue.

■ FABRIC

Fabric can be used to enhance woven jewelry. For instance, in the open twined project on page 76, it is used to fill the armature of the figure to add color and texture. You can leave the edges rough so that the fraying results in threads that escape between the open-twined areas.

■ BEADS

Use beads as accents on neck cords, connections, or threaded to make fringe. As you make jewelry, you'll find yourself collecting them, since they come in so many colors and finishes.

Bead, craft, and fabric stores all carry beads. Keep a selection on hand to choose from as you work. You can organize them by color, size, material, and purpose in see-through compartmentalized containers. When you're thinking about beads for a project, be sure that the holes are large enough to thread onto the material you plan to use. (Most beads are measured in millimeters, with the size referring to the diameter of the bead.)

Seed beads, which are added to weaving or threaded into strands of fringe, have a unique sizing system. Each size is labeled by number, and the larger the number, the smaller the bead. Size 11 seed beads are the most commonly used ones. Delica seed beads, imported from Japan, are cylindrical beads that come in a wider variety of colors than regular seed beads.

■ Beading Thread, Beading Needle, and Beeswax

If you make fringes with seed beads, you'll use beading thread and a beading needle. Prepare the thread with beeswax to keep it from tangling up as you work. The size you use will depend on the beads that you use.

Use a beading needle of a size that fits your thread and beads. Place the beads in a small shallow tray, bowl, or on a beading mat to hold them as you work.

GLUES AND FIXATIVES

Non-yellowing, or PVA glue, is used in many of the projects. It works well for adhering fibers, metals, and collaged paper. You can also use acrylic medium to adhere collage papers.

Use non-yellowing spray matte fixative to coat natural and found objects to keep the surfaces from flaking if you plan to use them as molds. Use fixative as a sealant for copper sheeting, mesh, and foil to help retain the color of the patina.

JEWELRY FINDINGS

Metal jewelry findings are used to finish a piece of jewelry so that it can be worn. They come in everything from 14K gold to brass to suit the piece of jewelry that you make. Whether you chose a precious metal or a less expensive alloy depends on the piece of jewelry you're making. Keep in mind that some alloys will darken the skin. The expense of a precious metal is well worth the money.

■ JUMP RINGS

These tiny wire circles with splits in them are used to connect various parts of jewelry.

They're available in precious metals or alloys such as gold, silver, plaited gold and silver, pewter, brass, and copper.

■ CLASPS

Clasps are attached to the necklaces or bracelets to hold them together. Basic spring-ring clasps work well for most pieces and come in precious metals and alloys. They are made of a ring with a small lever that, when pulled back, opens the clasp.

Elegant toggle clasps also come in various metals as well as many designs. Toggles consist of two parts, one piece attached to each end of a necklace or bracelet. One half of the toggle is a bar or narrow, elongated shape of some kind; the other half is a loop big enough for the bar to pass through so that when it is turned crosswise, it will hold tight. The simplest toggles have plain, straight bars and round rings.

■ BAR PINS

These pin backs have a flat, elongated piece on the back and a long pin for piercing fitted into a clasp that closes on the other end. They usually have three holes in the flat metal backing that make it possible to sew them to the back of a piece.

■ STICK PINS

These long pins have a little round piece on one end that makes it possible to glue them onto the back of a piece of jewelry.

■ EAR WIRES

Ear wires are attached to the decorative portions of earrings so that they can be worn. Purchase sterling silver or a hypoallergenic metal to prevent a reaction to the metal.

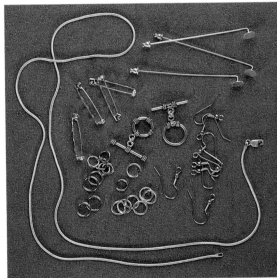

Findings: bar pins, stick pins, clasps, ear wires, and jump rings

When you've completed a woven necklace pendant, you'll add a neck chain or cord to it so it can be worn.

FINISHES FOR NECKLACES

In some cases, you'll want to use a commercial jewelry chain, especially if you're weaving with wire.

For the other projects in this book, you'll use plain, braided, or knotted waxed linen. If you wish, you can add beads and trinkets to the cord for embellishment. You can also attach the cord with a knot to a decorative loop made out of wire affixed to the top of the project. Two simple knots are used for neck cord connections: the Lark's head and an overhand knot.

If you're making a single-strand neck cord, I recommend using heavier 6- or 7-ply waxed linen. When you braid or half hitch the cord, use a more delicate linen of 4 ply or smaller.

LARK'S HEAD KNOT

The Lark's head knot (figure 1) is used primarily to connect single-strand neck cords to the top of a pendant that has a loop, usually made of wire (figure 2).

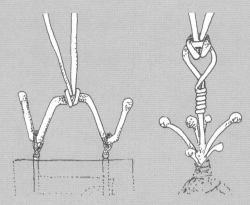

Figure 2

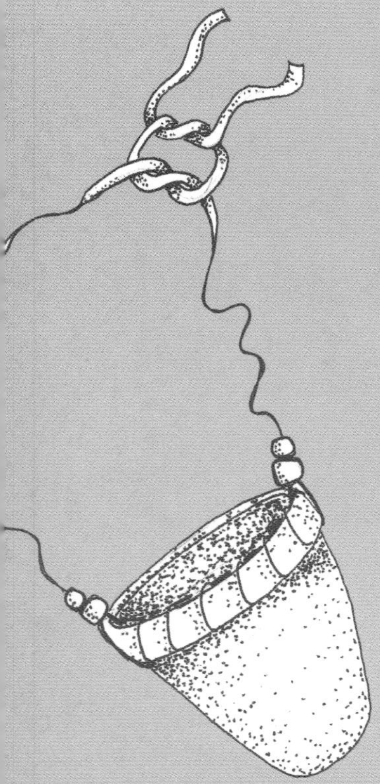

SINGLE AND DOUBLE OVERHAND KNOT

A single overhand knot (figure 3) is used to secure beads to a cord, leaving the ends of the cord as fringe.

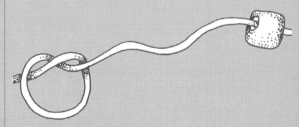

Figure 3

The double overhand knot is used to secure neck cords directly to the finished jewelry, whether metal or fiber. When you tie the knot twice (figure 4), it makes it very secure. This knot is also used to tie together two single strands of cord at the top of a necklace (figure 5, pictured on left side of this page).

Figure 4

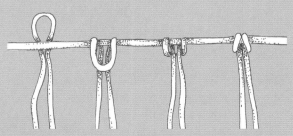

Figure 5

Figure 1

BRAIDED OR KNOTTED NECK CORDS

If you aren't using a single length of waxed linen as your neck cord, you can braid the cord or tie it with half-hitch knots.

To braid the cord, do the following:

1. Tie three lengths together using a double overhand knot (figure 6).

Figure 6

2. Braid the cords to a length of your choice, leaving tails that are about 4 to 6 inches (figure 7).

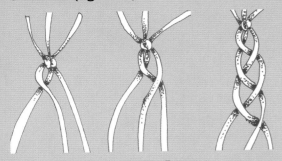

Figure 7

3. If you want to add decorative beads to the braided cord, thread them on as you braid it (figure 8).

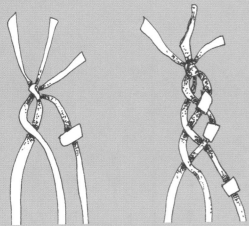

Figure 8

To make a half-hitched cord, do the following:

1. Tie two lengths of cord together using a double overhand knot. Loop the left strand over the right one and pull it through the loop (figure 9).

2. Reverse the direction of the knot to form the next link (figure 10).

3. Continue to alternate left and right to make the chain (figure 11).

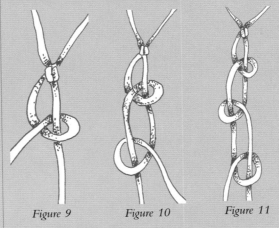

Figure 9   *Figure 10*   *Figure 11*

4. To add beads as you knot, thread them on (figure 12).

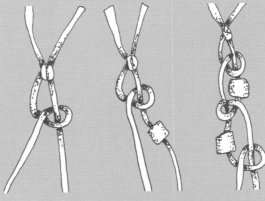

Figure 12

ATTACHING NECK CORDS

The double overhand knot is used in the following ways to attach cords directly to jewelry. If you plan to braid or hitch the cord, you can attach the cords to one side of the jewelry before braiding or knotting.

1. On a braided cord, treat two of the cords at the end of your braid as one, and thread them through the inside of the piece underneath the rim or into the woven work at the top of the body of the piece. On the outside of the piece, tie together the doubled thread and the remaining single thread with a double overhand knot, allowing the tails of the thread to hang as fringe (figure 13).

2. Thread through the two unknotted strands of a half-hitched cord and tie with a double over-hand knot, leaving two strands of fringe (figure 14).

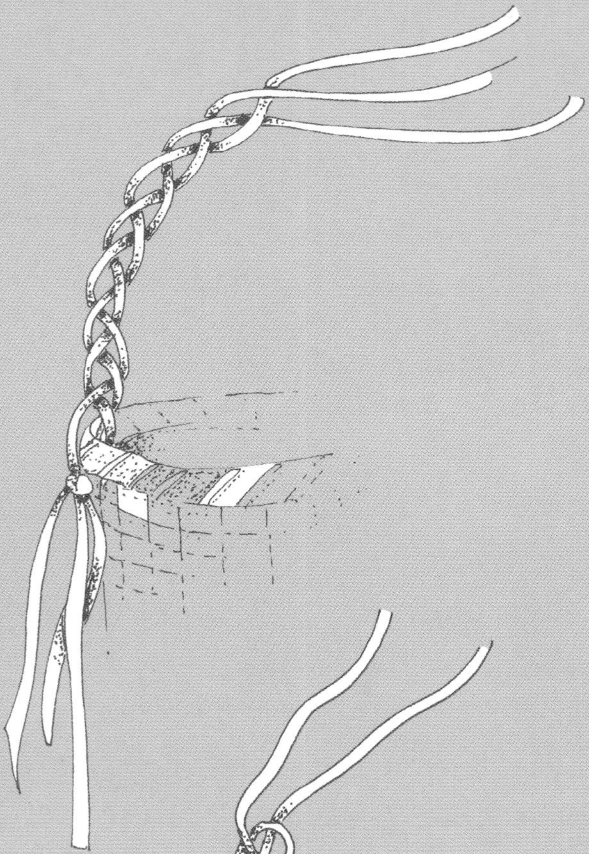

Figure 13

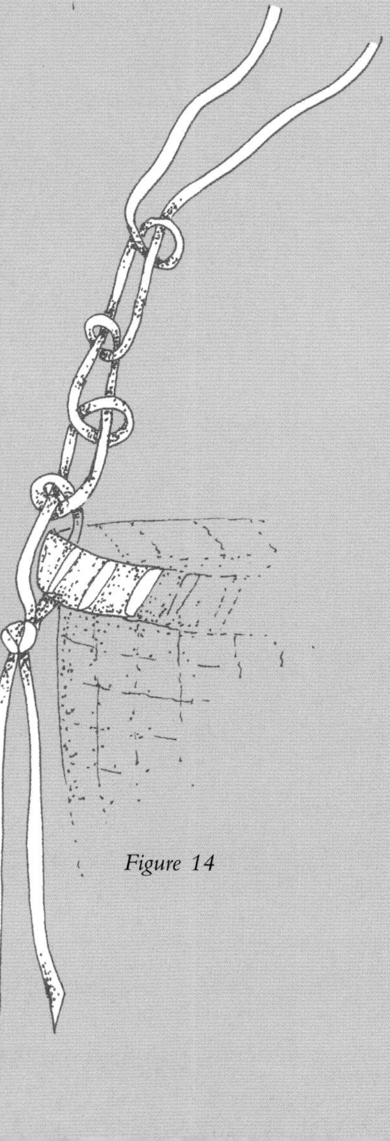

Figure 14

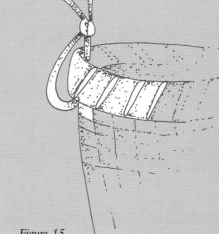
Figure 15

3. To connect a single strand, simply thread it through the rim or top and tie it with a double overhand knot to secure it (figure 15).

4. The single-strand cord can be embellished with beads (figure 16).

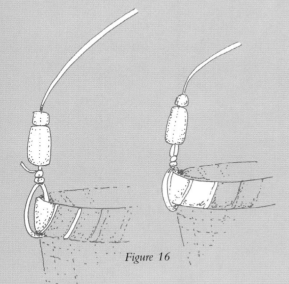

Figure 16

FRINGE

Fringe made from threads adds a nice touch to jewelry. Because they are made of two or three strands of multi-ply cord, the ends of braided and half-hitched cords (figure 17) can be untwisted to make a lightweight fringe.

Beads can be added to fringe by threading them on the cord and securing them by tying an overhand knot (figure 18). Tie a double overhand knot to hold beads with larger holes (figure 19).

When you're using single strand cords, tie an overhand knot at the top of the cord so it falls on the back of your neck. The ends of these threads can also be made into fringe, and you can also add small lightweight beads for more embellishment.

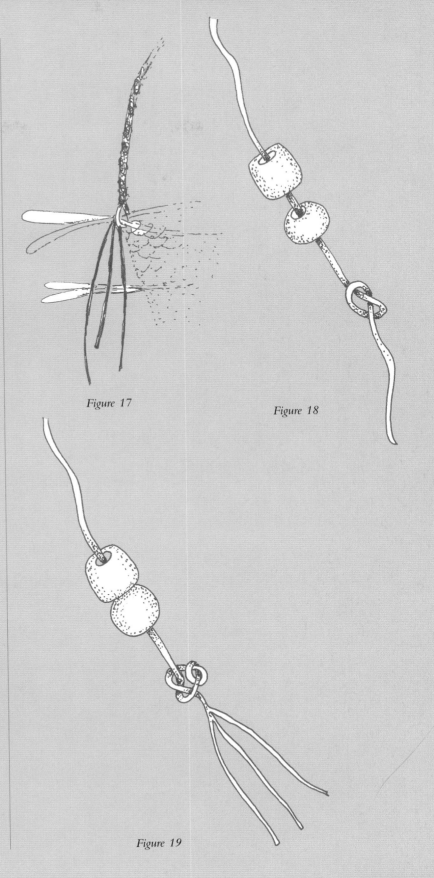

Figure 17

Figure 18

Figure 19

Tools and Equipment

Many craftsmen believe they can never have enough tools...or the more the better. But I take a more conservative approach. I limit my selection to a few functional, generic tools, and then add things as needed.

The basic tools needed to complete the projects in this book are explained in this section. The items needed for general purposes are very minimal, and most of the tools you need are for metalwork.

At certain points in the chapter you'll find descriptions of how to use the tools for applications such as forging and torching metal. Refer back to these sections when needed as you make the projects.

BASIC ITEMS

You'll frequently reach for the following things as you make woven jewelry. They're simple, but you'll miss them if you can't find them.

■ MEASURING TAPE OR RULER

Use for measuring lengths of materials, gauging distances between spokes, and any other measuring you need to do.

■ SPRAY BOTTLE

Fill this bottle with water, and use it to keep natural materials moist while you work with them.

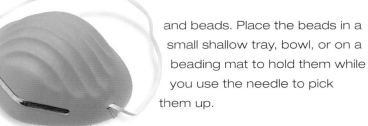

■ CLOTHESPINS

Clothespins come in handy for holding bark and other materials you want to shape into a mold while damp.

■ ADJUSTABLE SPRING CLAMPS

These clamps, with rubber tips, can be purchased at a hardware or home supply store. They are used to hold sections of jewelry together as you assemble it or secure metal pieces to the end of a table for drilling.

■ TAPESTRY NEEDLE

This needle is used to tuck spokes, lash on rims, loop and coil, connect neck cords to your piece, and attach pin backs.

■ BEADING NEEDLE

Use a beading needle to add beaded fringe to a piece of jewelry, such as a knotted pouch. Choose a size that fits your thread and beads. Place the beads in a small shallow tray, bowl, or on a beading mat to hold them while you use the needle to pick them up.

SAFETY EQUIPMENT

The following safety equipment is a must when you work with metals. You can buy all of these things at a home supply store.

■ SAFETY GLASSES

Wear eye protection whenever you work with metals, especially when forging or drilling. Bits of metal can shoot off in all directions. Buy glasses that are snug around the outside of your eyes so there's no possibility of a metal splinter slipping underneath the lenses.

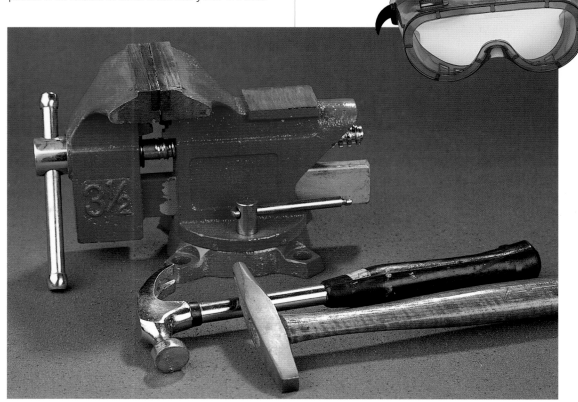

Hammer and anvil for forging metals

■ Dust Mask

Wear a dust mask when filing, drilling, and pounding metals to protect your lungs from metal particles.

■ Gloves

Always wear heavy gloves to protect your hands from getting cut when forging or drilling. Flexible leather gloves are perfect for this type of work.

■ Earplugs or Earmuffs

Wear ear protection to protect delicate eardrums when hammering metal. You can buy inexpensive earplugs at a drugstore, or use earmuffs from a home supply store.

TOOLS FOR PREPARING METAL

When you work with metal as a part of woven jewelry, you'll often forge the ends of wire or the edges of sheeting, shaping them to flatten them out so they're attractive and smooth. To add a colorful patina to copper or burn the ends of wire, use a simple propane torch.

■ Hammer and Anvil

A hammer and anvil are used for forging. Larger, heavier hammers are efficient for forging thicker sheet metals, while smaller hammers are used to forge the ends of wire. Jewelry hammers and anvils work well for this process, but regular hardware-store varieties of these tools are sufficient for the projects in this book.

FORGING METALS

Another way of finishing the ends of wire is to flatten them with a hammer and anvil to create smooth paddle shapes. Keep in mind that the wire will weaken a bit as it gets thinner, so don't overdo it, or the ends get brittle.

You'll also forge the edges of cut sheet metal to smooth them out, since even the highest quality cutters leave an edge that isn't appropriate for jewelry. Forging will leave a deckle edge that is organic looking.

As you work, allow the hammer to do the work. Position the head so that it will strike the area you're forging. Allow it to gain momentum as you swing it to disperse the weight and get optimum force. With practice you'll gain expertise and do this with ease.

You can finish the end of a cut piece of copper or silver wire by heating it in the flame of the torch. This not only produces beautiful coloration but smoothes the ends so they won't snag on clothing.

FINISHING THE ENDS OF WIRE

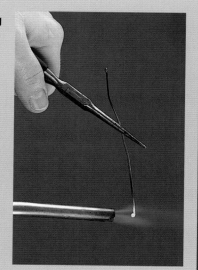

Place the end of the wire in the flame, and allow the metal to melt and ball up. Pull it from the flame when the end is shaped.

If copper wire is removed from the flame at the melting point and placed directly into cold water, it develops a bright red and/or pink cold-water patina that's permanent. If the shaped ends are air-dried instead of cooled in water, they'll turn black. If you burn the ends of silver wire and immerse them in cold water, they'll turn pale pink. If you torch the ends of tin-coated wire, they'll turn red and/or bright pink like bare copper, but remember to always do this outdoors because of the dangerous fumes released from the coating.

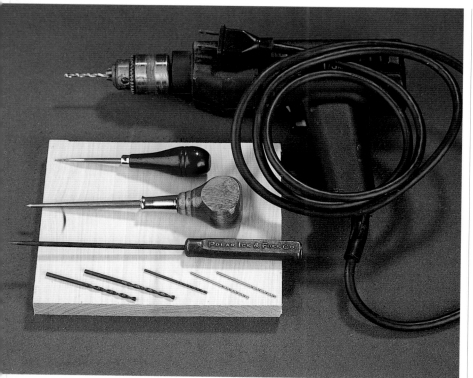

Top to bottom: drill, awls, drill bits, scrap wood

■ PROPANE TORCH

A propane torch, fitted with a propane tank, is used to heat up copper sheeting or mesh to produce coloration (see page 31). It is also used to apply heat to the ends of wires, as shown above, creating a nice rounded finish. This simple torch produces a large flame that burns fairly clean and hot. The standard tip that accompanies it is the perfect size for doing this type of metal preparation. The torch and replacement tanks can be purchased at home improvement and hardware stores.

PUNCHING AND DRILLING TOOLS

When you're working with sheet metal, you'll often need to drill holes for functional or decorative purposes. There are also times when you'll need to drill holes in wood pieces. A few simple tools are needed for this purpose.

AWL

Before drilling a hole in flat metal, use an awl to punch a smaller pilot hole in the metal so the drill won't slip when you use it. (Substitute an ice pick if you don't have an awl.) Use a hammer to tap the awl or ice pick to make the indentation. Make a pilot hole in a wood piece in the same way, if one is needed.

DRILL

Use a regular handheld drill fitted with a drill bit to drill through metal sheeting. Since you'll usually be fitting metal holes with standard $1/8$-inch eyelets, you'll probably use a $1/8$-inch drill bit.

When you punch or drill metal, clear off your worktable so you have plenty of room, then place a scrap of flat wood underneath the metal. A hard wood, such as hickory or oak, will hold up longer than a softer wood. You can get a piece of wood at a home supply store, or use a scrap left over from a wood-working project.

CUTTING TOOLS

You'll need some basic cutting tools for working fibers and wire. Whatever you pick, keep them clean and sharpened.

SCISSORS

Keep several pairs of scissors on hand for cutting waxed linen, floss, black ash, reed, and other weaving materials. For cutting copper foil, use a pair designated for metal only.

WIRE CUTTERS

Wire cutters are available in a wide range of prices and styles. I prefer side cutters and end-cutting nippers for cutting wire. Both of these tools are available at home

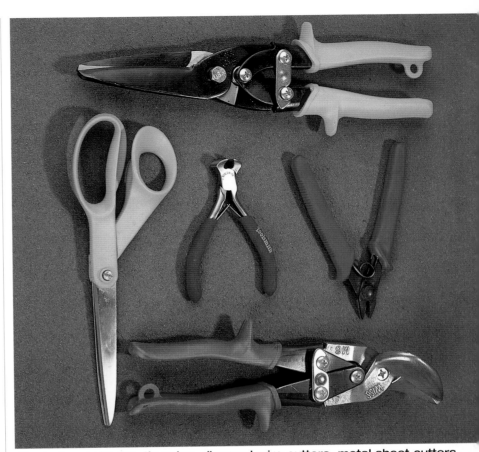

Clockwise: scissors, tin snips, diagonal wire cutters, metal sheet cutters, wire cutters

improvement or hardware stores, and they cut the wire close and clean, leaving a smooth end.

METAL SHEET CUTTERS OR TIN SNIPS

For the projects in this book that require cutting 18-gauge sheets of metal, use metal sheet cutters or tin snips. These cutters have flat blades that are designed for straight cuts or wide curves, and they leave a clean edge. The offset variety keeps your hands safely above your work. The tough molded plastic grips help you cut safely and comfortably.

Note: Avoid serrated cutters because they create a ridged edge that takes more time to forge and file down later.

MISCELLANEOUS TOOLS

The following tools are used for various metalworking purposes. You can find all of them at home supply stores.

■ FLAT-HEAD SCREWDRIVER OR CHISEL

When I first learned to work with metal, I used a saw to cut holes in copper sheeting. After breaking lots of blades, I decided to try something different. I learned that I could use a flat-head screwdriver or chisel to remove the metal. In the projects, you'll use this technique to cut a window from a piece of metal to make a small book.

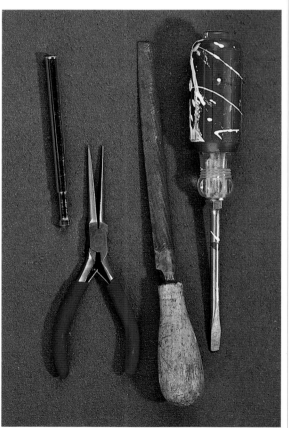

Left to right: eyelet-setting tool, needle-nose pliers, metal file, flat-head screwdriver

To do this, place the head of the tool along the line you wish to cut and tap the end of it with a hammer until you cut into the metal. Keep moving the head along this line, tapping the hammer, until you cut out the piece of metal.

■ METAL FILE

After you cut out a section of metal, you can fuse a round metal file to smooth the sharp edges. After you do this, forge the metal with a hammer and anvil until it's smooth. In general, it's a good idea to have a file on hand to smooth any rough edges that could snag clothing later on.

■ NEEDLE-NOSE PLIERS

Needle-nose pliers are used in a variety of ways when you're working with metal. Buy a pair that has no teeth or ridges that could leave marks on the metal. Use them to bend, pull, and handle copper foil and wire. In a way, they're like a second pair of hands. You'll also use these pliers to safely hold pieces of wire in the flame of a propane torch when you're finishing the ends. And when you need to pull apart a jump ring to attach it to a piece of jewelry, you'll need two pairs of pliers.

■ EYELET-SETTING TOOL

Eyelets function somewhat like grommets but are made of a single piece instead of two pieces. You'll use the accompanying setting tool to hold the eyelet in place while you roll down the backside of it. The process is very simple and adds a smooth finish to drilled holes in metal. You can buy this tool, along with eyelets, at a craft supply or scrapbooking store.

CREATING PATINA ON COPPER

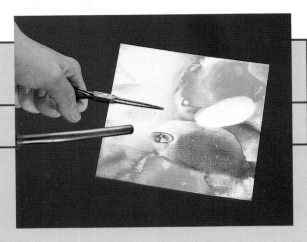

To color the surface of copper sheeting, mesh, or foil, flash it in the flame. Hold the material with pliers when you do this.

All of these materials react in a similar way in the flame, but the foil will color more quickly than the mesh because it's thinner. Don't overheat the thin metals, or you might burn holes through them.

Experiment to get different effects. For instance, by moving the material back and forth quickly in the flame, you'll get dark purples and pinks. If you focus the flame on one area, the copper will darken.

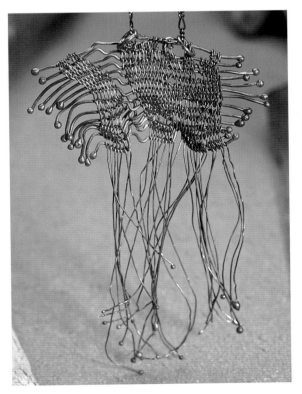

PLAITING

PLAITING IS THE FIRST BASKETRY TECHNIQUE
I LEARNED, AND IT IS THE BASIS FOR ALL OF
THE INTERLACED PARTS OF MY JEWELRY
DESIGNS. BECAUSE OF ITS SIMPLICITY AND
VERSATILITY, IT CAN BE USED TO WEAVE A
VARIETY OF MATERIALS TO CREATE JEWELRY.
IT CAN REFERENCE A SIMPLE OVER-ONE,
UNDER-ONE PATTERN (CALLED OVER/UNDER)
OR MORE COMPLEX PATTERNS BASED ON THE
SAME BASIC TECHNIQUE.

PLAITING

Figure 1

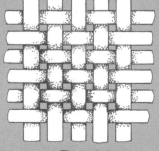

Figure 2

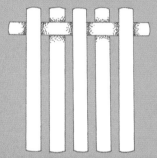

Figure 3

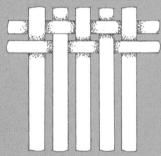

Figure 4

■ THREE OF THE FOUR PROJECTS IN THIS CHAPTER ARE MADE WITH A SIMPLE OVER/UNDER PATTERN. YOU'LL NOTICE THAT THE TWO BASKET PROJECTS INCORPORATE SIMPLE TWINING TECHINIQUES THAT ARE EXPLAINED LATER IN THE BOOK. THE FINAL PROJECT OFFERS YOU A CHANCE TO USE CONTINUOUS TWO/TWO TWILL FOR BEGINNERS, WHICH IS DESCRIBED IN THAT PARTICULAR PROJECT.

FLAT PLAITING

Weaving flat grids, or flat plaiting, is a technique commonly used to create bases or bottoms for baskets. Here, it is used to create the bases for the small baskets, or it is used to weave a flat piece that is made into jewelry. The over/under patterning forms a checkerboard design that shows off the materials. As you can already imagine, flat plaiting is highly adaptable to jewelry.

When plaiting is used to create the base of a basket, it is secured with twining so that the base holds its shape. The unwoven lengths of material are bent to form the spokes that are woven with new material, forming the sides.

The following illustrated steps show you how to weave flat plaiting. You can think of the vertical pieces as the weft and the horizontal pieces as the warp, since it emulates loom weaving.

1. Lay out the lengths of material in a vertical pattern, spacing them evenly (figure 1).

2. Thread a horizontal length through the vertical ones in an under-one, over-one pattern (figure 2).

3. Weave the second horizontal length over and under, opposite the weaving pattern of the previous row, creating a simple grid (figure 3).

4. Weave the remaining horizontal pieces, following the same pattern (figure 4).

5. If this grid is to be used as a flat base for a basket, hold the woven base in place with twined waxed linen (see page 58) to secure it (figure 5).

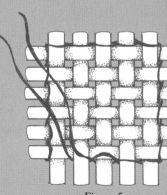

Figure 5

CIRCULAR PLAITING

If you're making a basket form, the flat plaited grid serves as the base of it. You'll stop the weaving at a certain point and bend up the unwoven lengths that extend from the grid to form the spokes. The spokes support strips of woven material called weavers. Together, the spokes and the weavers form the sides.

Circular plaiting is a general term that refers to weaving "around" the basket to build the sides and make it dimensional. In the projects, it's done with either a start-and-stop or continuous technique, both of which are explained next.

START-AND-STOP WEAVING

In start-and-stop weaving, every row uses a separate weaver that ends by overlapping on the beginning section of it. The end of the weaver is then trimmed and tucked behind a spoke to hide it and secure the row. Working from a grid base creates an even number of spokes. The weaver ends in the same over/under pattern, allowing the cut-off end to be concealed.

1. Begin a row by placing the end of the weaver on the outside of a spoke. Weave a simple over/under pattern (figure 6), continuing it all the way around.

2. When you reach the spoke where you began, weave over it. Then weave behind and over the next two spokes while you overlap the portion of the weaver already in place. At the fourth spoke, trim the weaver and tuck it behind the spoke (figure 7).

Figure 6

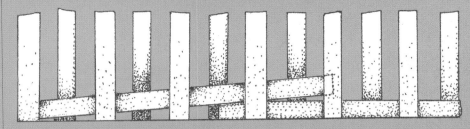

Figure 7

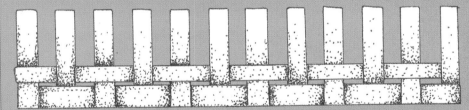

Figure 8

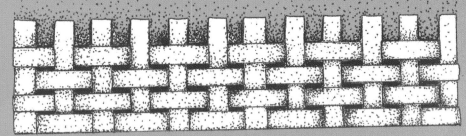

Figure 9

3. Use the same overlapping process and weave an opposite pattern on each consecutive row (figure 8).

4. Continue to weave until you build the wall of the piece (figure 9).

CONTINUOUS WEAVING

Continuous weaving involves using a length of material long enough to allow you to build the sides of the form without stopping and starting. In other words, one continuous piece of material is used to weave the rows on the basket form.

To make this work, you'll need an odd number of spokes. Since the base grid has an even number of spokes, you'll need to cut one spoke into two pieces before beginning to weave.

1. If possible, select a weaver long enough to allow you to weave continuously up the sides of the basket form without having to splice in new material. Before beginning to weave, use scissors to gradually taper 2 to 3 inches of the end of the weaver so that it ends in a point (figure 10). Tapering allows the material to fit tightly against the base.

2. Place the tapered or flexible end behind a spoke where you want to begin, and weave the material in the over/under pattern (figure 11).

3. Circle around to the point where you began. Because of the odd number of spokes, the weaving pattern will fall opposite the previous row (figure 12).

4. Continue weaving until your project is complete. To finish, taper the end of the weaver as you did when you began (figure 13). This allows for a gradual rather than an abrupt ending and looks more even to the eye.

Note: During the process of weaving, you can splice in another piece of material if you run out. To add a new weaver, first finish the current material by cutting the end of it and placing it on the outside of the basket on one spoke (figure 14). Add the new material by placing the end between the third spoke back and the weaving material, following the same weave pattern. This new weaver overlaps the end of the old weaver and will now take its place.

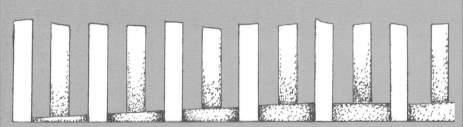

Figure 10

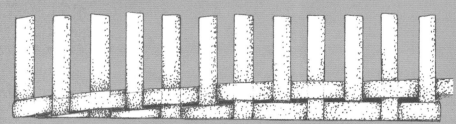

Figure 11

Figure 12

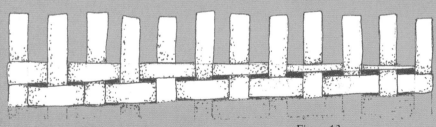

Figure 13

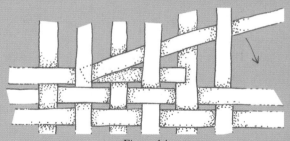

Figure 14

CUTTING AND TUCKING THE SPOKES

Cutting and tucking is a finishing technique used on many plaited baskets. At the end of the project, the spokes are cut and tucked back into the previous rows of weaving to create a nice clean edge that holds the rows in place.

Often a row or two of twining with waxed linen is added around the top between the spokes, which makes the cutting and tucking process easier. If you add twining, *all* the end spokes can be tucked inside the basket. If you *don't* add it, you'll need to trim the spokes that are on the outside of the basket so that they line up with the top edge of the basket.

The following illustrated steps show you how to cut and tuck a rim to create a nice finish around the edge of the basket.

1. Before tucking the spokes, soak the ends in water until they're pliable. Trim the ends with scissors on the diagonal, or cut them to resemble a picket fence. The ends need to be long enough to hide underneath a row or two of weaving inside the basket.

2. If you don't add twining around the top of the basket, bend every other spoke that falls behind a weaver over the top and into the weave on the other side (figure 15). Trim the remaining spokes with scissors.

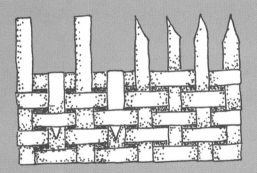

Figure 15

3. If you add twining, you can tuck every end. Bend each spoke inside the basket, over the twining, and back into the side weaving (figure 16). It's helpful to use a tapestry needle to open the inside weaving on small jewelry, allowing more space for the end of the spoke to slide in.

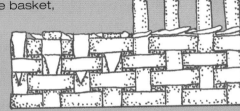

Figure 16

LASHING THE RIM

After the spokes are tucked in the top, you'll add an inside and outside rim to the edge to finish it.

1. Cut two rim pieces of the same length, each long enough to circle around the top edge and overlap two to three spokes (figure 17).

Figure 17

2. Use waxed linen as your lashing material. Tie the end of a length of it directly on the basket, at the top where the rim will be placed. Thread the other end of the lashing material with a tapestry needle (figure 18).

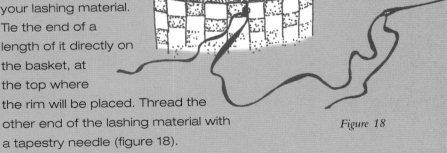

Figure 18

3. Use a whipstitch threaded between each vertical spoke to secure the rims to either side of the tucked top (figure 19).

4. End the lasher beneath the rim by stitching it several times to secure it and knot it in place.

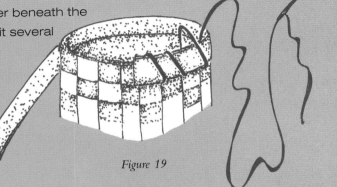

Figure 19

This impressive-looking piece of jewelry shows off simple plaiting. Birch bark strips contrast beautifully with the shiny patina of the copper. You can also use other materials as the contrasting weave. For ideas about this, take a look at the variations on page 45.

■ MATERIALS

1/16 to 1/8-inch-wide birch bark or other weaving material of your choice, 5 feet (weaver)

18-gauge copper wire, 7 inches (hanger)

4 pieces of copper foil, each 2 x 3 inches (weaver)

Cardstock (support)

24-gauge copper wire, 6 feet (loop)

4-ply waxed linen, 4 feet (neck cord)

2 decorative metal beads with large holes (embellishment)

■ TOOLS

Scissors

Measuring tape

Wire cutters

Metal sheet cutters or tin snips

Torch

Needle-nose pliers

■ TECHNIQUES

Finishing the ends of wire (see page 28)

Flat plaiting (see page 34)

Creating patina on copper (see page 31)

Finishes (see page 20)

■ INSTRUCTIONS

1. Use the scissors to cut the weaving material (birch bark or other) into 4-inch lengths.

2. Prepare the 18-gauge copper wire by burning the ends of it. Prepare the copper foil pieces by burning it with the torch to produce a patina. Cut the longer side of one of the 2 x 3-inch pieces of prepared copper into 1/8-inch-wide strips that end 1/4 inch from the edge of the foil (figure 1).

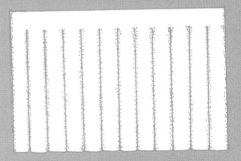

Figure 1

3. Beginning at one end of the cut foil insert, fold back the copper strips, alternating one left and one right until you reach the other end. Insert a length of birch bark or other weaving material and bend the strips back around it to enclose it (photo 1). Allow the excess material to stick out on either side.

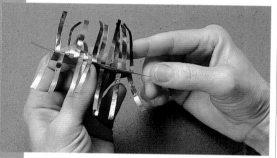

Photo 1

4. Place another length of weaving material inside the copper strips and enclose it to create the beginnings of the alternating over/under weave. Keep weaving in rows of the material (photo 2).

Photo 2

5. Weave until you reach a point where there is about 1/4-inch length of copper strip remaining.

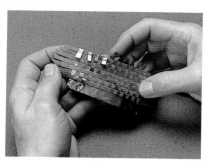

Photo 3

6. Fold down the copper ends onto the final row on the back of the piece, beginning with those that fall behind the last row (figure 2). Then fold the ones that fall on the outside of the last row down on themselves (photo 3).

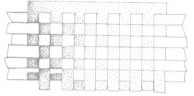

Figure 2

7. Trim the extended birch bark ends of the weaving material close to the edge of the grid (figure 3).

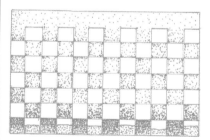

Figure 3

8. Use needle-nose pliers to fold the top portion of the uncut 3-inch side to the back of the grid.

9. Measure the grid, then cut out a piece of copper foil for the backing that's 5/16 inch larger than the grid all the way around. To eliminate the sharp edges, use needle-nose pliers to fold over the edges 1/16 inch all the way around. Start with the long edges, followed by the short edges (figure 4).

Figure 4

10. Cut a piece of heavy card-stock to the same dimensions as the grid. Place the paper on top of the folded copper backing. Position the plaited grid on top of the paper (photo 4).

Photo 4

11. Use needle-nose pliers to fold the long edges of the copper backing so they fit tightly around the front side of the grid's surface and the hidden card stock. Then complete the process by bending the two short ends over. Use the pliers to gently pinch the entire surface to create a flat piece (figure 5).

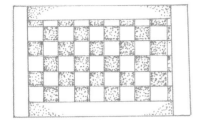

Figure 5

12. Cut off a 3-foot length of the 24-gauge copper wire. Bend it in the middle to form a loop. Hold the loop close to the top with pliers, and twist the wire with your fingers to form a closed loop (figure 6).

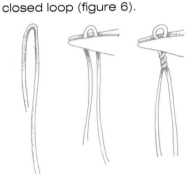

Figure 6

13. Place the loop at the top of the shorter end of the piece. Place one leg of the wire on top of the grid and the other on the back. Bend the front wire around the bottom of the rectangle to the back of the piece (figure 7). Crisscross it on the back wire as shown in figure 8.

14. Following figure 9, bring the front wire across the back horizontally and bend it up at a right angle before looping it over the top edge to the front.

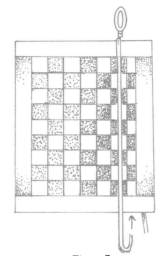

Figure 7

Figure 8

Form a loop that is about 3/16 inch long. Wrap the front wire around to the back again and thread it underneath the right-angled wire at the top. Pull it horizontally to the right side, and pull both ends to the front side so they meet.

15. Use needle-nose pliers to twist the loop at the top of the piece on the right side so it matches the one on the left side.

16. On the front of the piece, twist together the two ends of the wire (figure 10). Flatten the swirled wire to add embellishment.

17. Thread the 18-gauge prepared wire through the loops to make a hanger. Use pliers to bend one end of the wire into a curvilinear design of your choice (photo 5). Form a loop in the center, then shape the wire on the other side to match or compliment your design.

18. Fold the length of waxed linen in half. Attach it to the loop in the wire with a Lark's head knot.

19. Thread both ends of the waxed linen through the two beads. Pull the beads close to the wire. Tie an overhand knot on top of the beads to hold them in place.

20. Knot the ends of the neck cord together at the desired length.

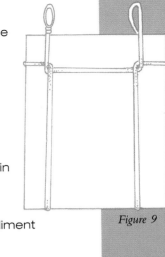

Figure 9

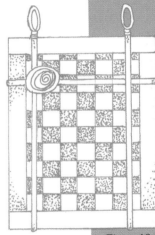

Figure 10

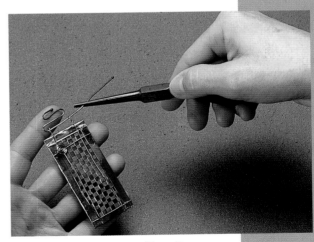

Photo 5

THE TRADITIONAL SHAPE OF A QUIVER BASKET
MAKES A LOVELY HANGING PENDANT. BLACK ASH,
BIRCH BARK, AND WAXED LINEN LEND IT TEXTURE
AND SUBTLE COLOR. BEADS ON THE NECK CHAIN
MAKE NICE DECORATIVE ACCENTS.

■ MATERIALS

1/8-inch black ash, 5 feet
(spokes)

4-ply waxed linen in black and
ochre, 5 feet each (weavers,
neck cord, rim lash)

1/16-inch black ash, 5 feet
(weaver)

1/16-inch birch bark, 2 feet
(weaver)

1/8-inch birch bark, 1 foot (rim)

Several decorative beads
(embellishment)

■ TOOLS

Spray bottle

Scissors

Measuring tape

Tapestry needle

■ TECHNIQUES

Twining a circular base (see page 56)

Continuous weaving (see page 36)

Circular twining (see page 58)

Cutting and tucking the spokes (see page 37)

Lashing the rim (see page 37)

Finishes (see page 20)

■ INSTRUCTIONS

1. Dampen the black ash to prepare
it for weaving by spraying it lightly
with water.

2. Use scissors to cut three lengths
from the 1/8-inch black ash, each 10
inches long. Find and mark the centers. Lay them out flat with the center
marks crossed to make a round base
that resembles bicycle spokes.

3. Cut off a 40-inch length of the black waxed linen. Loop it in half, and twine one row around the base while the piece is lying flat. Lift up the base and hold it. Continue to twine three more rows. As you do this, gradually bend the lengths of material away from you, forming six spokes for the sides.

4. Use scissors to cut five of the six spokes in half lengthwise, forming 10 spokes. Thin the sixth spoke so it matches the 10 spokes. Now you have an uneven number of spokes or 11. Place your index finger in the basket to give it support and shape as you continue to work (photo 1).

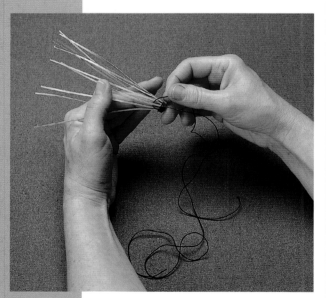

Photo 1

5. Dampen the spokes again to keep them pliable. Use black waxed linen to twine for two rows between each of the 11 spokes. Cut one length of the black waxed linen, and add in ochre twine of the same length as the remaining black length. Begin to twine using the black and the ochre for a total of four more rows. You'll notice that the pattern spirals due to the odd number of spokes.

6. Use a continuous weave to add six rows of the $1/16$-inch black ash.

7. Cut off one 30-inch length of black waxed linen and one 20-inch length of the ochre. Add them in and twine four rows. When you've completed four rows, cut the ochre linen and replace it with a length of black linen as long as the one with which you're weaving. Continue to twine for three more rows before cutting and ending both of the black pieces (photo 2).

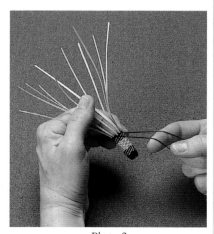

Photo 2

8. Continuously weave $1/16$-inch birch bark for 12 to 15 rows.

9. Cut a 36-inch piece of black waxed linen. Loop it over a spoke so that 12 inches is on one side and 24 inches is on the other. Twine three rows, and then cut off the shorter black piece. Replace it with a length of ochre waxed linen of the same length as the remaining black piece, and continue the pattern of twining for four more rows, creating the spiral again.

10. Add six rows of the $1/16$-inch black ash.

11. Repeat step 7.

12. Weave three rows of $1/16$-inch black ash, and finish the sides by adding a single row of twining with the 4-ply waxed linen.

13. Cut and tuck the top of the basket.

14. Cut two rim pieces from $1/8$-inch birch bark, each about $1 1/2$ to 2 inches long. Thread a tapestry needle with black waxed linen, and lash on the rim.

15. Add a plain black waxed linen neck cord to the top of the basket. String on several decorative beads to the waxed linen cord to sit on top of the basket.

VARIATIONS

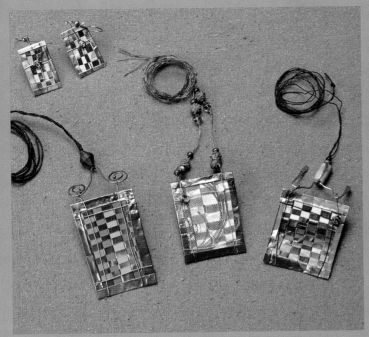

WOVEN COPPER NECKLACES AND EARRINGS

COPPER BOOK NECKLACES

QUIVER-SHAPED NECKLACES

BASKET NECKLACES

This unique necklace combines bookmaking, basketry, and metalwork. The simple book form is assembled with cold connection jewelry techniques. The wire grid is made with flat plaiting.

■ MATERIALS

18-gauge copper sheeting, at least 2 x 5 inches (covers)

24-gauge copper wire, 5 feet (weaver)

Brass or metal eyelets (embellishment)

Small pieces of card stock, handmade paper, or decorative paper (pages)

2 medium-size jump rings (connections)

18-gauge copper wire, 4 inches (loop)

7-ply waxed linen, 4 feet (neck cord)

Decorative metal bead with hole large enough to fit over doubled waxed linen (embellishment)

■ TOOLS

Measuring tape

Metal sheet cutters or tin snips

Safety glasses

Hammer and anvil

Torch

Scrap piece of hardwood

Flat-head screwdriver

Awl

Handheld drill and $1/16$-inch and $1/8$-inch masonry or metal drill bits

Metal file

Wire cutters

Eyelet-setting tool

Scissors

Needle-nose pliers, 2 pairs

Small paper hole punch (optional)

■ TECHNIQUES

Forging metals (see page 27)

Creating patina on copper (see page 31)

Flat plaiting (see page 34)

Finishing the ends of wire (see page 28)

Finishes (see page 20)

■ INSTRUCTIONS

1. Use metal sheet cutters or tin snips to cut out two matching pieces of copper sheeting that measure about $2 1/2$ x $1 1/4$ inch each. Use the cutters to taper the length of the pieces to form an uneven, interesting shape. These pieces will become the covers of your small book.

2. Before hammering the metal, put on safety glasses to protect your eyes. Prepare the edges of the copper book covers by forging them with a hammer and anvil to create an organic, irregular edge. Torch-fire the pieces to give them a pretty patina.

3. Place the front cover on top of a scrap of wood. Cut an elongated window in the cover by placing the flat-head screwdriver along the edge of the shape you want to cut before hammering the end of it (photo 1). The opening you create will be rough.

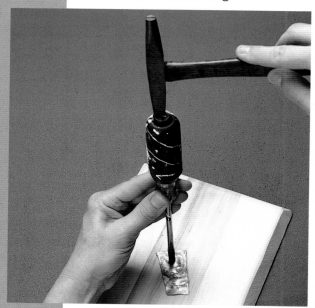

Photo 1

4. Punch holes about ¹⁄₈ inch apart around the outside edge of the window with the awl and hammer (photo 2). Then use the drill fitted with the ¹⁄₁₆-inch drill bit to drill the holes. When

you're done, hammer out the rough edges and file the holes, if needed.

Photo 2

5. After the window is cut out and removed, forge the sharp edge with the hammer and anvil. Use a metal file to file off any remaining sharp edges (photo 3).

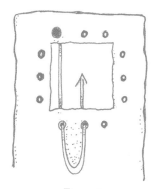

Photo 3

6. Use wire cutters to cut off a 3-foot length of 24-gauge wire. To create a knot that holds the end of the wire in place on the back, bend a small wire swirl in it or burn it to make a ball that you flatten slightly with the hammer and anvil. Thread the wire through a hole from the

back of the copper sheet book cover to the front (photo 4).

Photo 4

7. Start the grid by threading the wire through all the holes vertically, just as you would set up a flat plaited grid for plaiting (figures 1 and 2). Once the vertical wires are in place, plait the

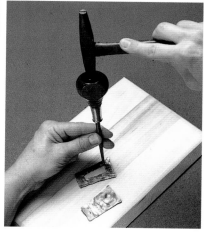

Figure 1

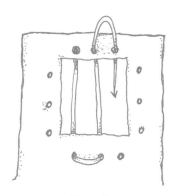

Figure 2

grid horizontally with the same piece of wire, threading each hole, creating an over/under interlaced woven flat grid (figures 3 and 4).

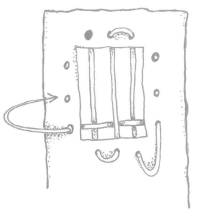

Figure 3

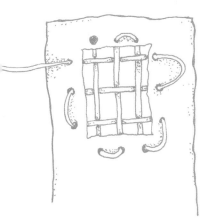

Figure 4

8. When the weaving grid is done, end the wire by swirling it in a small tight circle inside the book cover to complete it (figure 5).

9. Mark both the cover piece and the other matching piece of copper at the two top corners about ¼ inch in from both the sides and the top. These

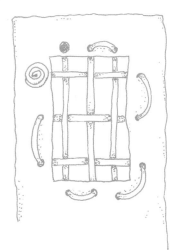

Figure 5

marks indicate where you'll place the eyelets.

10. Place the awl on each of the marks and tap it with the hammer to make indentations in the metal. Use a hammer and awl or a drill fitted with the ⅛-inch bit to make the holes.

11. Following the directions provided by the manufacturer, use the eyelet-setting tool to insert the eyelet in the holes (photo 5).

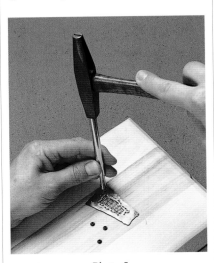

Photo 5

12. Cut several pages from various papers to fit inside the cover. Position the front cover on top of them and mark where holes need to be made. Use the awl or a small paper hole punch to create the holes.

13. Use the needle-nose pliers to assemble the book with the two jump rings (photo 6).

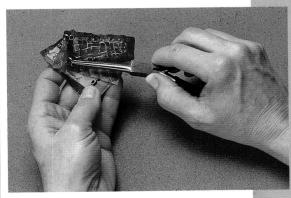

Photo 6

14. Burn the ends of the 18-gauge piece of wire. Bend half of it into a decorative shape (see the project on page 38). Thread the other straight end through the jump rings, and bend the central area into a subtle loop. Then bend the other end of the piece into a decorative shape.

15. Fold the waxed linen in half and use a Lark's head knot to tie it to the center of the loop. Thread a decorative bead on both strands of the linen and secure it with a knot at the top. Tie the ends of the linen together to form a neck cord in the length of your choice.

THIS SMALL BLACK ASH BASKET IS MADE WITH A SIMPLE TWILL WEAVE. TWINED WAXED LINEN HOLDS THE ASH IN PLACE, MAKING IT EASY TO HANDLE AS YOU WEAVE THE SIDES. A PIECE OF WOOD ADDED AS AN ACCENT ON TOP LENDS THE NECKLACE A RUSTIC LOOK.

■ **MATERIALS**

1/8-inch black ash, 9 feet (spokes and rim)

4-ply waxed linen, 21 feet (weavers, lashing material, neck cord)

1/16-inch black ash, 14 feet (weavers)

Small piece of hard driftwood or piece of thin branch (embellishment)

2 silver beads (embellishment)

■ **TOOLS**

Spray bottle

Scissors

Measuring tape

Pencil

Tapestry needle

Handheld drill

1/8-inch drill bit

Jigsaw or handsaw (optional)

Sandpaper (optional)

■ **TECHNIQUES**

Flat plaiting (see page 34)

Circular twining (see page 58)

Continuous weaving (see page 36)

Cutting and tucking the spokes (see page 37)

Lashing the rim (see page 37)

Finishes (see page 20)

■ **INSTRUCTIONS**

1. Before you work with any of the ash in this project, dampen it by spraying your hands with water from the spray bottle and gently running each piece through your wet fingers.

2. From the 1/8-inch black ash, use scissors to cut nine 9-inch lengths and one 11-inch length. Set aside the remainder for the rim.

3. Cut off a 42-inch length of waxed linen.

4. Lay out the nine lengths vertically, spaced 1/16 inch apart. Use the measuring tape and a pencil to lightly mark the center points (figure 1).

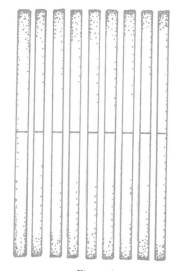

Figure 1

5. To twine the base, fold the long piece of waxed linen in half and loop it over the end length on the left, just above the pencil mark. (As you twine,

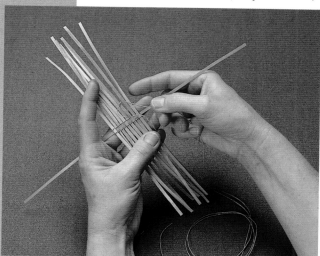

Photo 1

you can hold the lengths in your hand or keep them flat on the table. Do whatever is easiest for you.) Twine horizontally through the nine lengths just above the marked center point. Flat plait the 11-inch black ash length over and under the nine vertical pieces, following the center marks. Rotate the base and continue to twine around the small woven area on the other side (photo 1). Stop twining where you began. Don't cut the waxed linen.

6. Use the spray bottle filled with water to lightly dampen the base. Bend both the vertical and horizontal lengths away from yourself with the pencil marks on the outside. Now you have 20 spokes for supporting the weavers that will form the sides of the basket. Continue to twine with the same piece of waxed linen for three more rows around the sides so there are a total of four rows on this first area of twining. You've now completed the base.

Photo 2

7. Cut the center spoke on one of the long sides in half lengthwise to create an odd number of spokes (photo 2).

8. Cut a 30-inch length of 1/16-inch black ash and taper the end of it to a point. Begin a continuous weave (photo 3). Weave a total of six rows.

Photo 3

9. Cut off a 36-inch length of waxed linen. Loop the center over the central back spoke to begin continuous circular twining. Twine three rows.

10. Next you'll weave a 2/2-twill pattern. To do this, cut off a 7-foot weaver from 1/16-inch black ash. Taper the end to a point, and lay in the piece to begin continuous weaving as you did in step 8. It's simple—instead of weaving over and under each spoke, you'll weave over two spokes and under two.

11. Continue with this twill pattern for 18 to 21 rows, and finish it by tapering the end of the

Photo 4

weaver before you tuck it in (photo 4).

12. Cut off a 36-inch length of waxed linen, loop the center over the middle back spoke, and use continuous circular twining to weave three rows.

13. Cut a 30-inch length of 1/16-inch black ash, and taper the end of the ash before weaving six rows.

14. Twine three more rows of waxed linen as you did in step 9.

15. To finish the sides of the basket, cut and taper a 20-inch length of 1/16-inch black ash, and weave three rows with a continuous weave.

16. To finish the top, cut off a 12-inch length of waxed linen and twine one row around the top of the basket before you cut and tuck the spokes (figure 2). Use the tapestry needle to help open up the weaving as you tuck in the spokes.

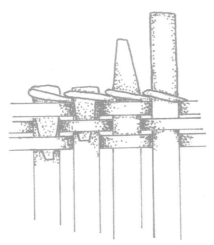

Figure 2

17. Cut two 1/8-inch black ash rim pieces, each approximately 4 inches long. Cut a 24-inch length of waxed linen. Thread the tapestry needle and lash on the rim (photo 5).

Photo 5

18. Measure the longer width of the top of the basket, and drill two holes in the small piece of driftwood or branch that are spaced apart the same distance. When you position the wood over the top, the holes should fall close to these outer edges.

19. Cut off a piece of waxed linen that's 4 feet long. Thread the two silver beads on the linen, and push the ends through the holes in the wood. Tie each end of the linen directly around each side area of the rim, and secure them with a couple of square knots. Allow the beads to fall on top of the basket when you hold up the necklace (figure 3).

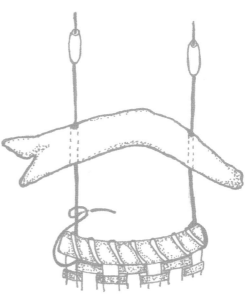

Figure 3

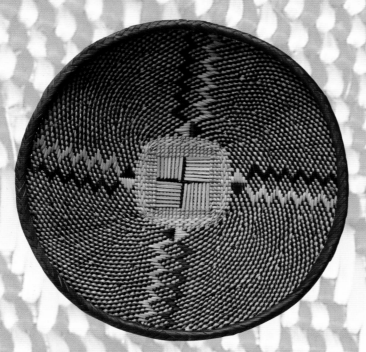

TWINING

TWINING IS ONE OF MY FAVORITE BASKETRY TECHNIQUES BECAUSE IT'S EXTREMELY RELAXING AS WELL AS VERSATILE. THERE ARE LOTS OF VARIATIONS OF TWINING, BUT THIS SECTION COVERS THE ONES THAT WORK WELL FOR SMALL PIECES.

TWINING

■ ALL OF THE TWINING PROJECTS USE A TWO-STRAND TWINING TECHNIQUE THAT IS VERY BASIC. ITS APPEARANCE VARIES DEPENDING ON THE MATERIALS AND SHAPING. YOU'LL BEGIN WITH A WEAVER LOOPED AROUND THE END OF A SERIES OF SPOKES. AS YOU TWINE, THE WEAVER HOLDS THEM IN PLACE. IF YOU TWINE TIGHTLY, THE SPOKES WILL BE EVENLY SPACED. ONCE THE SPOKES AND WEAVERS ARE IN PLACE, TWO-STRAND TWINING IS BASICALLY THE SAME, WHETHER CIRCULAR OR FLAT.

MAKING A CIRCULAR BASE

For these projects, you'll begin the base of the piece using one of two methods. You'll do this portion of the twining on a flat surface. Eventually, you'll pick up the base, bend the spokes away from you, and begin twining the sides.

SINGLE-SPOKE BASE

This type of base works well if you're using larger or more rigid materials. You'll notice that lots of baskets have this type of base and construction. The spoke count is established at the beginning and varies from piece to piece.

1. To begin, cross the spokes at their centers so they're evenly spaced like the spokes on a wheel. Loop a weaver over one of the spokes (figure 1).

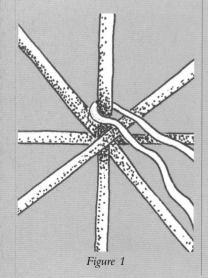

Figure 1

2. Twine between each of the spokes individually (figure 2). (See page 58 for more information about twining).

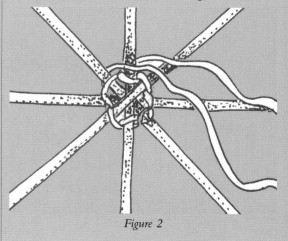

Figure 2

MULTIPLE-SPOKE BASE

This method works well if your project requires many spokes to create a tighter weave on a piece and give it a smaller diameter (such as an elongated pouch). You'll begin by grouping and tying the spokes into one complete set before it's divided up as you twine, until you eventually twine single strands.

1. To begin, cut a weaver and find the center. Use a double overhand knot to tie the weaver around the center of the group of spokes, bundling the spokes together (figure 3).

2. Divide the two sets that you've tied together into four. Begin with four groups of spokes and twine between each bundle (figure 4).

3. As you twine, you'll separate each group of spokes into two again so that you are working with smaller bundles. The tension, material, and size of the base determine when you do this. As the base becomes larger, you will ultimately twine the spokes individually (figure 5).

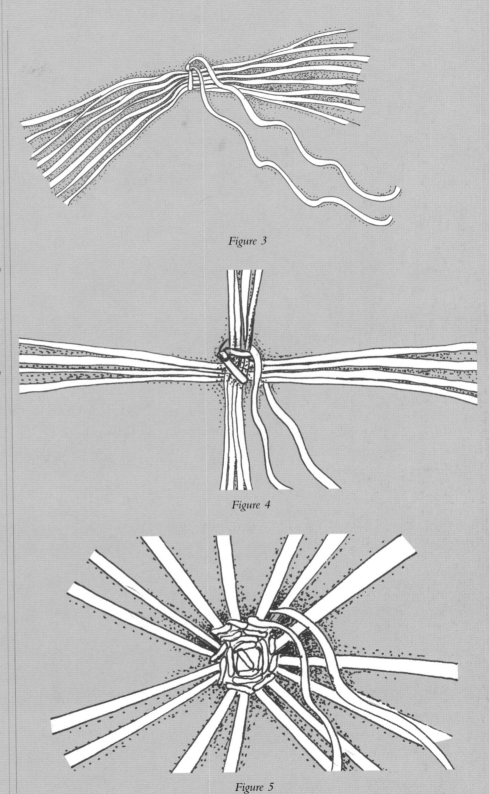

Figure 3

Figure 4

Figure 5

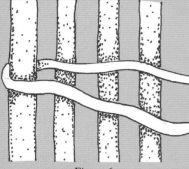

Figure 6

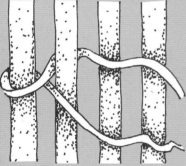

Figure 7

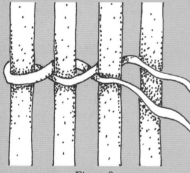

Figure 8

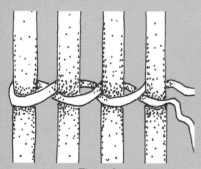

Figure 9

BEGINNING TO TWINE

You'll start both continuous and flat twining by working with two strands of material.

1. Fold the weaver in half and loop it over the first spoke (figure 6). You now have two strands, or weavers, with which to work.

2. Twist the two lengths around the adjacent spoke (figure 7).

3. Continue to twine around the spokes, keeping the tension even (figures 8 and 9).

CIRCULAR TWINING

After you've established the base, continuous circular twining is used to form dimensional pieces with sides. Naturally dimensions vary from project to project. Pack the twining firmly around the spokes as you weave (figure 10). Make certain the spokes are always vertical and don't pull to one side.

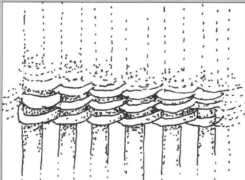

Figure 10

FLAT TWINING

Flat twining is very simple. You'll weave across a row of spokes before turning the piece around and twining back to the other side (figures 11 and 12).

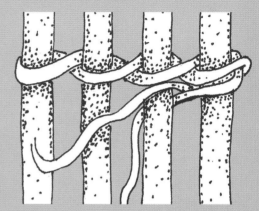

Figure 11

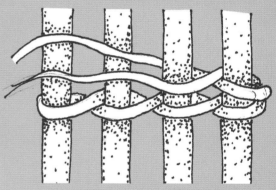

Figure 12

OPEN TWINING

The term open twining is descriptive of weave that features rows of regular twining with space left between them that allows the spokes to show (figure 13). You'll twine continuously, spiraling up if you're making a circular piece or simply weaving back and forth if you're making a flat one.

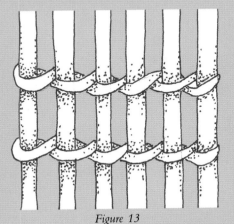

Figure 13

As you work, you can add full twists between the spokes that serve to separate as well as secure them (figure 14). Twisting the weavers assures that the spokes won't shift or move. Separating the rows of twining and then the spokes creates even tension and strength in the weaving.

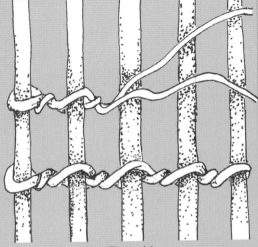

Figure 14

DECREASING THE NUMBER OF SPOKES

Decreasing the number of spokes allows you to decrease the diameter of a piece in order to shape it. For instance, you'll do this when you taper the top of a pouch.

The most efficient way to get rid of a spoke is to twine it together with the adjacent spoke before cutting it off above the previous row of twining. When you continue twining, the cut end will be buried.

1. Twine the spoke that you want to remove with the one adjacent to it (figure 15). Do this for as many spokes as you wish to remove.

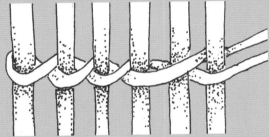

Figure 15

2. After you've twined a couple of rows, trim the spokes you wish to remove, reducing the bulk and leaving one spoke (figure 16).

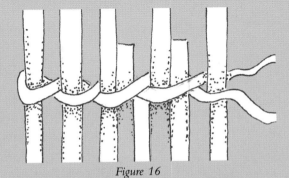

Figure 16

ADDING AND ENDING WEAVERS

Unless you're making a very small project, you'll eventually have to add more material as you twine. Or you might want to add in a new color.

If you add another color and your piece has an even number of spokes, the two colors will simply stack on top of each other, row after row. If your piece has an odd number of spokes, the two colors will spiral upward.

The following steps detail this process. The illustrations reflect views from inside the basket.

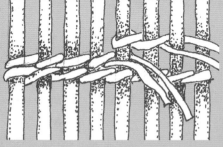

Figure 17

1. If the material is too small to simply tuck underneath the twining, trim the ends of the weavers that you're done with and place them inside the piece. Loop a new weaver on the spoke where the twining stopped, then begin twining again (figure 17).

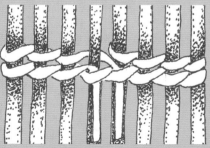

Figure 18

2. If the ends of the material are long enough to tuck inside the project, then tuck them underneath the twining on the back or inside the piece on adjacent spokes. Add another weaver and continue twining on the second spoke, where you tucked the second end (figure 18).

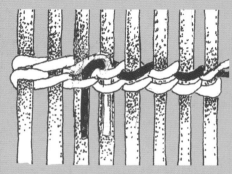

Figure 19

3. If one weaver ends before the other one, you can add a single weaver by tucking the end of the short one underneath the twining on the back or inside of the piece. Add a new length (shown tucked at beginning in black) by securing it under the twining. Then twine with the existing weaver and the new one (figure 19).

ENDING THE TWINING

When you've finished twining, end the weavers by simply cutting both of them and tucking them on the back or the piece or inside it (figure 20).

Figure 20

After you've done this, you have several options for finishing the spokes. Sometimes you'll simply leave the spokes as they are since they're a part of the design of the piece. For instance, if you used heavy wire that has been hammered on the ends to form decorative spokes, you'll leave the ends showing.

If you've used other materials, such as waxed linen, you can leave the spoke material hanging as fringe. Or, if you want a clean finish around the edge of a pouch or other rounded piece, you can trim the spokes and them tuck them inside. You can tuck one row or several, depending on your design. Several rows will create a thicker rolled border. There are many ways to do this, but the variation described here is the one used in the projects.

1. Work from the outside of the piece, with the spokes up. Choose a spoke to begin with and fold it behind the adjacent right spoke (figure 21).

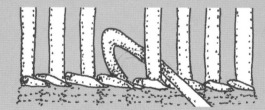

Figure 21

2. Continue this process with the next spoke. Loosen the first tucked spoke slightly with a tapestry needle to create a small loop, and leave it there for later (figure 22).

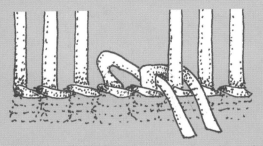

Figure 22

3. Continue to tuck all the way around, keeping the tension consistent (figure 23).

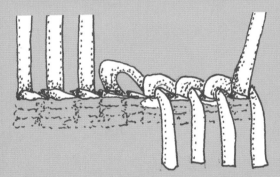

Figure 23

4. When you reach the beginning spoke, tuck the final spoke through the loop (figure 24).

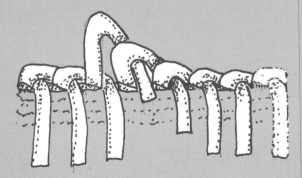

Figure 24

5. Pull the last spoke into place to complete the process (figure 25).

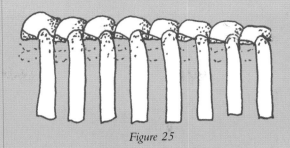

Figure 25

6. If you want to tuck a second row, continue with the same process, leaving a loose loop at the beginning. Then loop the folded-in spokes on top of each other (figures 26 and 27).

Figure 26

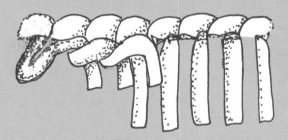

Figure 27

Various colors of waxed linen twined around spokes of reed result in this festive patterned pouch. Plaiting and twining techniques are combined to complete this piece.

■ MATERIALS

$^{11}/_{64}$ flat oval reed, 15 feet (spokes, rim)

Waxed linen in rust, sage, orange, salmon, yellow, and light brown, 15 feet each (weavers)

Waxed linen, 5 feet in color of your choice (neck cord)

Accent beads (embellishment)

■ TOOLS

Scissors

Measuring tape

Spray bottle

Tapestry needle

■ TECHNIQUES

Flat plaiting (see page 34)

Beginning to twine (see page 58)

Circular twining (see page 58)

Cutting and tucking the spokes/plaiting (see page 37)

Lashing the rim/plaiting (see page 37)

Finishes (see page 20)

■ INSTRUCTIONS

1. Cut the reed into 12 lengths, each 12 inches long, to form the main spokes of the basket. Cut one 14-inch length for the center spoke. Mark the centers on the oval side of the spokes.

2. Soak the reed in water for about 20 minutes to make it pliable. Fill the spray bottle with water so you can keep the material damp while you work with it.

3. To begin the base, place the 12 lengths of reed in a vertical position on a flat surface with $1/16$ inch between each of them.

4. For the weavers, cut each of the six colors of waxed linen into 5-foot lengths. Fold one of these pieces with a 2-foot-long strand on one side and a 3-foot long strand on the other side. Loop it over the first spoke on the far left (figure 1). Since the ends of the linen are different lengths, they will run out at different times, creating a pattern as you weave in new colors.

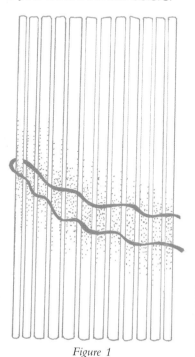

Figure 1

5. Twine across the centers of the spokes (figure 2) until you reach the other side. Plait the 14-inch piece of reed (the center spoke) directly beneath the twined row, and continue twining all the way around the spoke with the waxed linen (photo 1).

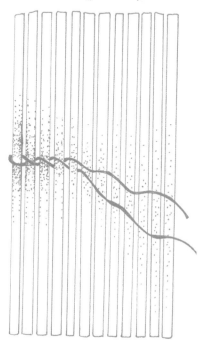

Figure 2

Photo 1

6. Spray the reed lengths with water to keep them pliable and bend them away from you with the oval side out (photo 2).

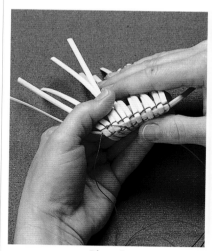

Photo 2

7. You now have a total of 26 spokes. Continue to twine, beginning the sides of the piece (photo 3).

Photo 3

8. After twining several rows on each side, taper the spokes on both sides to slightly reduce the width of each (photo 4). As you twine, the pouch will pull in gradually toward the top.

Photo 4

9. When you run out of the first length of waxed linen, cut and tuck it inside the twining before replacing it with another color of waxed linen (photo 5).

Photo 5

10. Continue to add a different linen color each time you run out of one, and the patchwork pattern will form. Make the pouch shorter or longer, depending on your preference.

11. When you end the twining, use the tapestry needle to open up the twining, and cut and tuck the spokes.

12. Cut two pieces of flat oval reed to fit the inside and outside diameter of the top of the basket, plus about 1/2 inch for overlap. Lash these pieces to the rim using a tapestry needle threaded with waxed linen.

13. Finish the neck cord with a loose half-hitch cord.

14. Slide the accent beads onto the cord so they'll fall on either side of the top of the basket. Use a tapestry needle to attach the cord to the rim.

VARIATIONS

MULTICOLORED POUCHES

FRINGE

BECAUSE EMBROIDERY FLOSS COMES IN SUCH A WIDE RANGE OF COLORS, YOU CAN CREATE A BEAUTIFUL GRADUATED PATTERN WITH TWINING. BEADS THAT CASCADE OVER THE TOP OF THE POUCH REFLECT THE STEPPED PATTERN OF THE STITCHING.

■ MATERIALS

6- or 7-ply brown waxed linen, 20 feet (spokes and neck cord)

Black, brown, dark red, burnt orange, ochre, tan, and white embroidery floss, 5 feet of each color (weavers)

Size 11 black seed beads, 5 grams (fringe)

Beading thread, 10 feet (fringe)

Brown waxed linen (neck cord)

2 glass beads (embellishment)

■ TOOLS

Scissors

Beading needle

Tapestry needle

■ TECHNIQUES

Multiple-spoke base (see page 57)

Circular twining (see page 58)

Ending the twining (see page 60)

Finishes (see page 20)

■ INSTRUCTIONS

1. Cut 16 lengths of brown waxed linen, each 15 inches long. Use the 5-foot length of black embroidery floss to bundle the lengths of linen together, beginning a multiple-spoke base. Tie the floss so one length (or weaver) is about 20 inches long and the other is 40 inches (photo 1). This difference in length will create the patterning in the finished piece.

Photo 1

2. Twine the base for about 16 rows, dividing the number of spokes as you work. You'll begin to see the formation of a pouchlike shape around row 10, which is also approximately the point at which you'll begin twining around individual spokes instead of multiple spokes.

3. Cut off the shorter black weaver when you've completed about 16 rows. Cut the 5-foot brown floss in half, and add in one length of it where the black weaver ended. Now twine with a black and brown weaver, combining these colors for approximately six rows (photo 2).

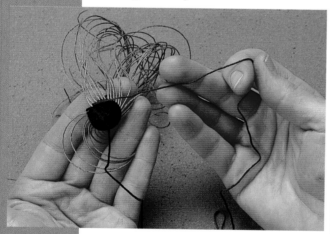

Photo 2

4. After you've twined these rows of combined color, add the other 30-inch brown floss weaver to the existing brown one, and twine the two brown weavers together for four rows.

5. Cut the 5-foot piece of dark red floss in half. End the shorter brown weaver before adding the dark red weaver. Twine together the brown and red floss for four rows.

6. When you get to the end of the dark red weaver, add the next 30-inch-long pieces of embroidery floss of another color. Twine for four rows. To create the pattern, continue to add the rest of the colors in this way, twining four rows at a time.

7. Finish the spokes of the piece with a tucked border.

8. Thread the beading needle with about 5 inches of the beading thread, leaving the longer length hanging. Push the needle through the front of the pouch underneath the rim, and pull the 5-inch length through to the inside. Remove the needle, and tie the tail to the longer thread with a double overhand knot to secure it to the rim. Once it is secure, trim the tail inside the pouch. Thread the needle back onto the thread in preparation for beading.

9. Thread on a length of seed beads and pull them down the side of the piece, stitching back through the pouch so no thread is visible (figure 1).

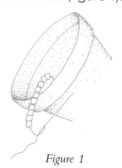

Figure 1

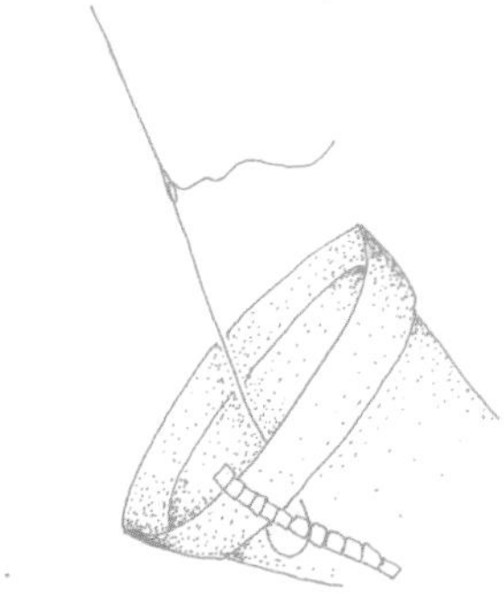

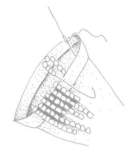

Figure 2

Figure 3

Anchor longer rows by tacking them down with thread (figure 2). Stitch back inside the pouch, and repeat, adding rows of different lengths (figure 3).

10. Continue beading around the top of the pouch, adding rows of varied lengths, and anchoring them as needed (figure 4).

11. Cut a length of brown linen into a neck cord, and thread on the two glass beads. Use a tapestry needle to attach the cord to the sides of the pouch.

Figure 4

TAPERED POUCH STICKPIN

THE USE OF NARROW WAXED LINEN RESULTS IN A TIGHTLY TWINED PIECE. BRIGHT COLORS UPDATE THIS TRADITIONAL BASKETRY TECHNIQUE.

TECHNIQUES

Multiple-spoke base (see page 57)

Circular twining (see page 58)

Adding and ending weavers (see page 60)

Decreasing the spoke count (see page 59)

Ending the twining (see page 60)

MATERIALS

3- or 4-ply light green waxed linen, 15 feet (spokes)

3-ply light green waxed linen, 10 feet (weaver)

3-ply light purple waxed linen, 10 feet (weavers)

Stickpin with round head (finding)

TOOLS

Scissors

Tapestry needle

Instant-bonding glue

Photo 1

INSTRUCTIONS

1. Cut the green waxed linen into 16 spokes, each 10 inches long.

2. Set up the spokes for a circular twined base. Use the 10-foot green weaver to bundle them together in the center, then separate them into four equal groups. Begin twining, and as you work, keep dividing the rows as you did in the project on page 66. Eventually the piece will cup up, and you'll be twining around single spokes. You'll weave about 15 to 20 rows of the light green to form the base (photo 1).

3. When you've finished the base, cut one of the green linen threads. Cut off 5 feet of purple waxed linen and add it in where you cut off the green thread. Twine with the two colors for two rows.

4. Twine around two spokes as you begin the third, reducing the spoke count to alter the pattern. Twine the fourth row with the same reduced spoke count.

5. Switch back to the full spoke count on the fifth and sixth rows. Reduce the spoke count again by one on the seventh and eighth rows. Continue this pattern of switching back and forth until you've twined

12 to 14 rows. When you're done, cut the green weaver and add in a 5-foot dark purple one. You'll now be twining with two purple weavers. Twine about 15 rows, then reduce the spoke count by one to begin tapering the pouch.

6. Keep twining and decreasing the pouch every few rows. When you reach about row 26, insert the round head of the stickpin between the spokes. Twine a couple of rows around it to secure it, and put a small dot of glue on the inside to anchor it to the inside wall of the pouch. (Photo 2 shows the back of the finished pouch with the stickpin intact.)

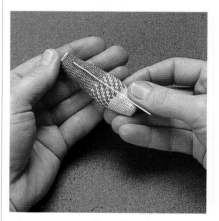

Photo 2

7. Continue to twine about four more rows before tucking the spokes to create a neat finished border.

TWINED SILVER PIN WITH BEADS

FORGED PIECES OF SILVER WIRE TWINED FLAT WITH THINNER SILVER WIRE SERVE AS A FOIL FOR A SPARKLING ARRAY OF BEADS ON THIS PIN.

■ TECHNIQUES

Forging metals (see page 27)

Flat twining (see page 58)

■ MATERIALS

18-gauge silver wire, 20 to 25 inches (spokes)

26-gauge silver wire, 7 feet (weaver)

Triangular seed beads (size 11), 5 grams (embellishment)

Bar pin back with holes (finding)

■ TOOLS

Wire cutters

Measuring tape

Hammer and anvil

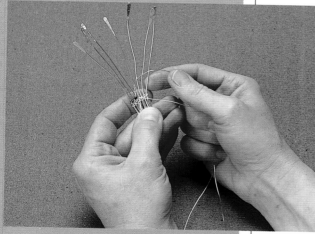

Photo 1

■ INSTRUCTIONS

1. From the 18-gauge wire, cut seven pieces, each 2 to 3 inches long, varying their lengths slightly. Forge their ends.

2. Arrange the seven spokes horizontally. Cut a 6-foot length of the 26-gauge wire. Fold the wire in the center.

3. Loop the wire over the end spoke before twining through the seven spokes (figure 1).

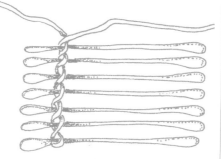

Figure 1

4. Turn the piece around and twine back across (photo 1).

5. After twining three full rows, begin adding beads by threading a single bead onto one of the wires. Let the bead fall to the pin, and position it on top of the spoke as you twine around it. Add a bead to every other spoke (figure 2).

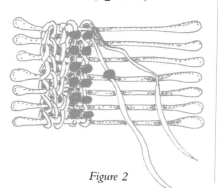

Figure 2

6. Continue to twine, adding beads until you reach the other side. Finish off the piece with several rows of bare wire to reflect the beginning of the grid (photo 2).

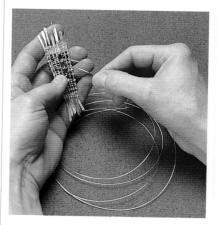

Photo 2

7. Cut and anchor the end of the wire into the previous row, on the back side of the piece.

8. By hand, thread both ends of the 12-inch length of 26-gauge silver through the front of the twined flat grid in the center, and pull the ends out the other side so they're equal in length. Thread through the holes of the pin back and position it on the back of the piece. Secure it with stitching that follows the direction of the twining. When it is secure, stitch the ends a couple of times in and out of the grid, and trim the wire.

TWINED COPPER BAG NECKLACE

THIS FAIRLY SIMPLE PROJECT ALLOWS YOU LOTS OF CREATIVE LATITUDE NOT ONLY IN ITS DESIGN BUT FOR THE ENCLOSURES YOU CHOOSE TO PUT INSIDE. SMALL STONES, BEADS, TUMBLED GLASS, FOUND OBJECTS, OR OTHER MATERIALS SHOW THROUGH THE SHINY COPPER NETTING.

■ MATERIALS

18-gauge copper wire, 30 inches (spokes)

24-gauge copper wire, 6 feet (weaver)

4-ply waxed linen (neck cord)

■ TOOLS

Wire cutters

Safety glasses

Torch

Scissors

Needle-nose pliers

■ INSTRUCTIONS

1. Cut the 18-gauge copper wire into five 5-inch lengths and one 8-inch length. Put on safety glasses, and use the torch to burn the ends of the wire.

2. Hold the six spokes in the center, aligned at the top so the longer piece of wire extends further at the bottom.

3. Find the midpoint of the 24-gauge wire and anchor it by wrapping it back over itself. You'll now have two lengths of wire to use for twining (photo 1).

4. Bend the spokes into a radial shape, and use the weaver to begin open twining between them (photo 2). Cup the shape away from yourself as you begin to twine.

5. Open twine spokes for approximately four rows, cupping the shape as you work. While the bag is still open, place the objects inside and continue to twine (photo 3).

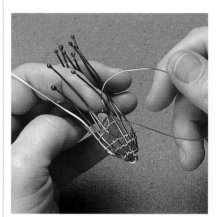

Photo 3

6. As you progress up the spokes, do less twisting between them to pull in the shape (photo 4).

Photo 1

Photo 2

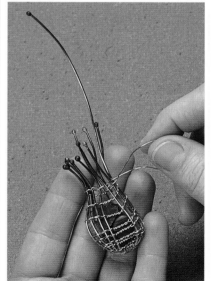

Photo 4

7. When you reach the top, twist the wire, wrapping the spokes together (photo 5).

Photo 5

8. Use the longer protruding spoke to make a loop to hold the necklace, wrapping the wire back on itself at the loop's base (photo 6).

Photo 6

9. For a neck cord, cut a piece of waxed linen in the length of your choice. Bend the linen in half, and thread the looped portion through the copper loop. Push the ends of the threads back through the linen loop, and pull the cord tight.

VARIATIONS

TWINED BAG NECKLACES

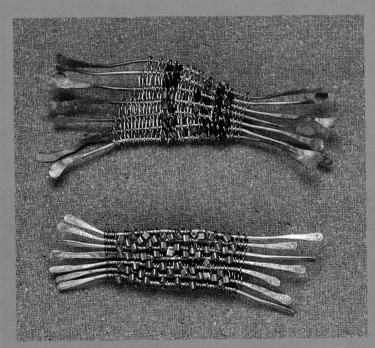

TWINED PINS WITH BEADS

Using copper wire, fabric, and some imagination, you can make your own version of this whimsical figurative pin. Follow the basic instructions, but feel free to lend it your own touches.

■ MATERIALS

22-gauge copper wire, 7 feet (spokes and connections)

24- or 26-gauge copper wire, 25 feet (weaver)

Multicolored fabric scraps, 1 x 3 inches (embellishment)

Copper mesh, 5 x 2 inches (embellishment)

Large round bead (figure's head)

Stickpin with rounded end (finding)

■ TOOLS

Wire cutters

Safety glasses

Torch

Awl

Needle-nose pliers

Instant-bonding glue

■ TECHNIQUES

Finishing the ends of wire (see page 28)

Creating patina on copper (see page 31)

Open twining (see page 59)

■ INSTRUCTIONS

1. For the arm and leg spokes, cut 10 pieces of 22-gauge wire, each 5 inches long. Put on your safety glasses, and use the torch to burn the ends of the wires. Burn a patina on the copper mesh.

2. Group five of the ten spokes together to start the arms. Hold the spokes together about 1/2 inch from one end. Cut off a 6-foot length of 24- or 26-gauge wire to serve as the weaver for the arms. Find the center of the weaver, and wrap the wire around the end to secure it.

3. Open out the spokes, and begin to open twine around them with the wire (photo 1). Twine approximately four rows.

Photo 1

4. Tear or cut the piece of fabric into small bits. Use an awl to push a bit of the fabric into the opening in the twined wire (photo 2). Twine three more rows and pull the tension to close the center of the spokes, creating the first arm.

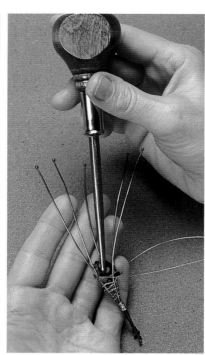

Photo 2

5. Use open twining on the remaining length of the spokes on the other side of the spokes, creating a second arm. Fill it with bits of fabric, pull the wire to close it, and wrap the wire to close the ends.

6. Use the remaining five spokes to make the legs, following the same steps that you used to make the arms. Use the needle-nose pliers to bend the forms in the middle so they emulate legs.

7. Cut a 10-inch length of 22-gauge wire and use it to connect the arms and legs together, leaving about 1 inch between them for the body (photo 3).

Photo 3

8. Cut three 10-inch-long pieces of 22-gauge wire. Use the torch to burn the ends of each of the 3 pieces of wire. Thread the unburned ends through the large bead that will be the head. Anchor the ends of the wire by randomly securing them in the body of the figure (photo 4).

Photo 4

9. Fold in the piece of copper mesh 1/8 inch along the edges to eliminate the sharp edges. Fold the mesh in half and gather the ends together. Shape and mold the mesh between the legs, and pull the gathered ends over the arm and up to the neck area (photo 5). If the mesh is too long, trim it down with scissors. If it is too bulky to gather up the ends, cut small triangular sections from the edges.

Photo 5

10. Cut a 4-foot length of 26-gauge wire and bend it in half. Loop the center of the wire around the neck, just underneath the head. Wrap around the neck area approximately 10 times, with both lengths to secure the mesh. End both wire ends on the back side of the figure.

11. Use the instant-bonding glue to attach the stickpin to the mesh on the back of the figure.

12. Twist the two wire ends coming out of the wrapped neck together. Keep twisting them and bring the wire downward towards the stickpin. When you reach the top of the stickpin, twist the wire around

Photo 6

it (photo 6). Continue to twist the wire a couple of times, ending in the center of the back of the figure.

13. Bring the wire ends around the front of the figure, and swirl both pieces of wire together snugly around the figure's waist as if it were a belt (photo 7). Cut the ends of the wire and tuck them behind the swirl.

Photo 7

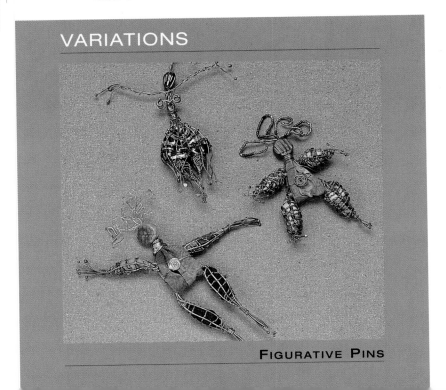

VARIATIONS

FIGURATIVE PINS

THIS ARTISTIC BRACELET IS TWINED WITH COPPER WIRE WOVEN OVER SPOKES OF COPPER BURNED TO PRODUCE A BEAUTIFUL PINK PATINA. EVEN THOUGH THIS PIECE OF JEWELRY LOOKS RICH, IT IS NOT EXPENSIVE TO MAKE.

■ MATERIALS

18-gauge copper wire, 9 feet (spokes)

24-gauge or smaller copper wire (weaver)

Copper jewelry clasp (finding)

24 medium-size copper jump rings (finding)

■ TOOLS

Wire cutters

Torch

Safety glasses

Needle-nose pliers

■ TECHNIQUES

Finishing the ends of wire (see page 28)

Flat twining (see page 58)

■ INSTRUCTIONS

1. Cut 65 to 75 pieces of 18-gauge copper wire for the spokes. The bracelet shown fits a small wrist and contains 65 spokes, which are broken into segments of five each. Seventy spokes work well for a medium-size wrist, and 75 or more for a larger wrist.

2. Use the wire cutters to cut the wire into spokes ranging in size from 1 inch to 1¼ inches. Burn the ends of the wire to create the pink coloration.

3. Lay out the spokes in groups of five (figure 1), positioning the various sizes so that you have a slightly uneven edge.

4. Cut off a 40-inch length of the narrow copper wire to use as the weaver for the spokes. Twine five spokes together (photo 1).

Photo 1

5. When you reach the other side of the spokes, stop in the middle of the section and finish it by threading the ends of the wire into the previous row of twining (photo 2).

6. Continue twining the remaining sections (figure 2).

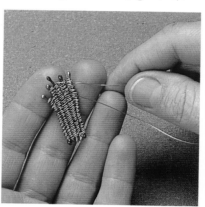

Photo 2

7. Use the needle-nose pliers to open the jump rings and connect the segments in two places between the outermost spokes on either side (photo 3). Attach the clasp to one side and another jump ring to the other side.

Photo 3

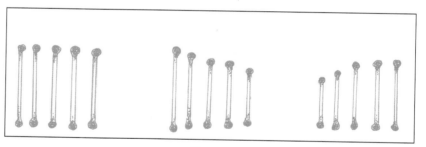

Figure 1

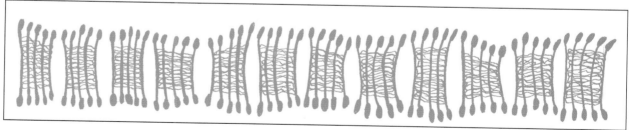

Figure 2

VARIATIONS

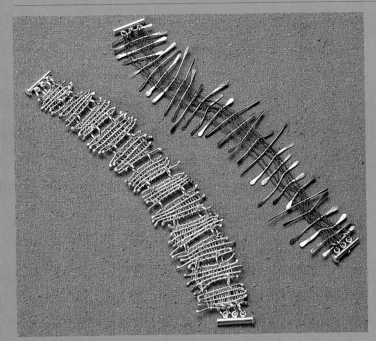

TWINED SPOKES BRACELETS

FIGURATIVE PINS

TWINED POUCHES WITH BEADED FRINGE

TAPERED POUCH STICKPINS

LOOPING

LOOPING IS A SIMPLE STITCHING TECHNIQUE THAT'S EXTREMELY VERSATILE AND ADAPTS WELL TO JEWELRY. IN THE FOLLOWING PROJECTS, YOU'LL LEARN HOW TO CREATE DIFFERENT EFFECTS USING CIRCULAR LOOPING ON A MOLD OR FLAT LOOPING OFF OF ONE SUPPORTING PIECE. YOU CAN USE DIFFERENT MATERIALS, VARY THE STITCH COUNT, OR CHANGE THE TENSION OF THE STITCHING TO MAKE EACH PIECE UNIQUE.

LOOPING

MOLDS AND FRAMES FOR LOOPING

There are many variations of looping. In the projects in this book, circular looping is attached to a dimensional mold that is either temporary (removed after it is used to shape the piece) or permanent (left intact to serve an integral part of the jewelry). Flat looping is begun on a horizontal piece that supports the stitching and remains as a permanent part of the piece.

If you're using thread, you'll secure the tail before threading it through a tapestry needle. If you're using rigid wire, you don't have to use a needle but can manipulate it with your hands.

TEMPORARY MOLD

A temporary mold determines the size of a circular looped piece. You can enlist lots of ordinary things to use for this purpose. For instance, an empty toilet paper or paper towel roll is the perfect diameter for shaping a pouch necklace. When the mold is removed, the piece drapes, retaining the mold's size.

Before you begin, tie the end of the looping material around the mold, leaving a 4-inch tail that you can make into fringe later if you want. You'll attach the first row of looping to this grounded material (figure 1). From there, you'll add more rows. This technique works well for all temporary molds.

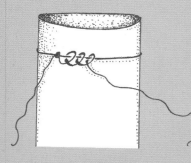

Figure 1

PERMANENT MOLD

A permanent mold becomes an integral part of circular looping. Smooth rocks, small pieces of smooth driftwood, found metal objects, shaped bark, and seedpods are examples of permanent molds. Any small object is appropriate as long as it's not sharp and can be worn.

You'll attach the looping material to a permanent mold with the same basic method as a temporary mold (figure 2). However, in this case, you must make certain the attachment is as secure as possible, since the mold will become a part of the jewelry.

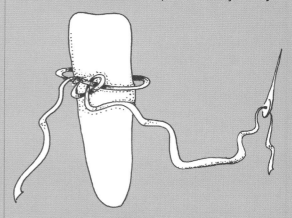

Figure 2

If the mold has a hole in it, you can tie the end of the material through the hole to anchor it and make it secure. If your mold has an irregular or tapered shape, you can take advantage of it by beginning to loop where there's a smaller diameter. As you continue looping, the material will be held in place as you work.

You can also do circular looping on a framelike structure incorporated into the piece. In the project on page 104, you'll see an example of a structure built from wire that is both functional and decorative. This structure determines the size, shape, and direction of the looping. Use heavy gauge wire, sticks, bamboo pieces, or other rigid materials for this purpose.

You'll begin flat looping the same way. To attach the material, tie it with a square knot onto the horizontal piece (figure 3) and leave a tail hanging. You can add fringe later on or bury the tail underneath the looping (see page 91).

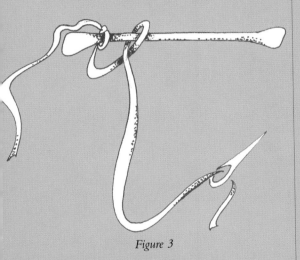

Figure 3

CIRCULAR LOOPING

Once the looping material is attached to the mold or other structure, the process of circular looping is very simple. You'll repeat the same stitch to create a series of rows that are joined together to make body of the piece.

1. To begin, use a tapestry needle or your fingers to push the looping material underneath the part that is attached to the mold. Loop it behind and back over itself, leaving a loose loop. Continue to loosely loop the thread (figure 4).

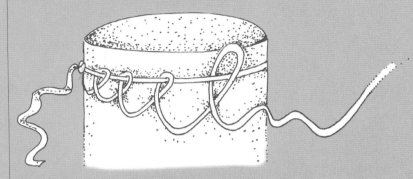

Figure 4

2. After you finish looping the first row, begin looping stitches off of the previous row. Pull the material to create a loop size of your choice. As you work, make sure the loops are consistent (figure 5).

3. Continue looping around the entire frame, adding each row of stitches to the previous one (figure 6). The tension, size, and number of stitches will vary according to the project.

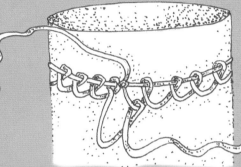

Figure 5

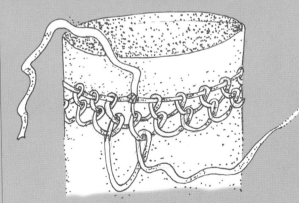

Figure 6

FLAT LOOPING

Flat looping starts on one straight structural piece, such as a round dowel or a length of heavy wire. This piece provides a hanger for the stitching. From this point, you can continue the looping back and forth, adding one row to the next. To do this, you'll simply loop across the initial piece, then flip the whole piece over and loop back across.

1. Loop the first row directly on the area of the supporting structure where you want to begin the looping (figure 7). Make the loops even and consistent both in size and spacing.

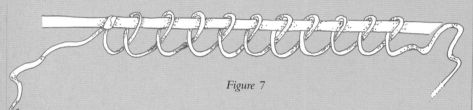

Figure 7

2. After the first row is on the frame, reverse the orientation of the frame so you can add the next row of looping onto the first row (figure 8). Continue this process of reversing the frame to add rows of looping until you reach the desired length.

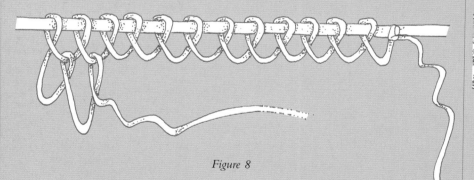

Figure 8

ADDING MATERIALS TO LOOPING

If you're using flat looping, you also have the option of incorporating other pieces of material into the stitching to add both visual and structural interest. You can use rigid or flexible materials, whether natural or man-made. Bark, ash, reed, and wire are just a few examples.

To do this, place the material at the bottom of the last looped row and hold it in place while you loop around it, catching it in the previous row of stitching. Keep adding pieces of material as desired (figure 9). In general, the looping should hold the material fairly tight.

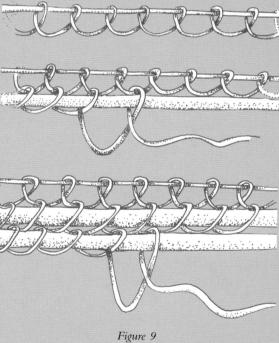

Figure 9

SPLICING

This section explains how to splice, or add in, more looping material if you run out or want to change colors.

FIBER

To splice in thread or fiber, you'll join together the ends of the thread to connect them. Begin by separating the strands that you want to connect about 1 inch on each end of the threads (figure 10). Then cut away about half of the strands, so the joined-together ends are the same thickness as the thread (figure 11).

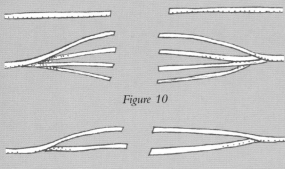

Figure 10

Figure 11

Twist or roll the two ends back together (figure 12). As you continue to work, treat this joined area carefully so you don't pull the connection apart. Now you can continue looping without interruption. If the thread won't ply together sufficiently, use the method of splicing described next for nonfibrous material.

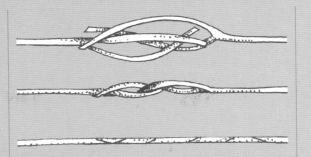

Figure 12

NONFIBROUS MATERIAL

To splice in a nonfibrous material, such as wire, begin by concealing the end of the material you're working with in the previous rows of looping (figure 13). To do this, stitch back, following the exact looping pattern. Carefully trim the end of the material. Add new material using the same technique: Work one end into three to four loops in the previous rows. Continue looping with the new material.

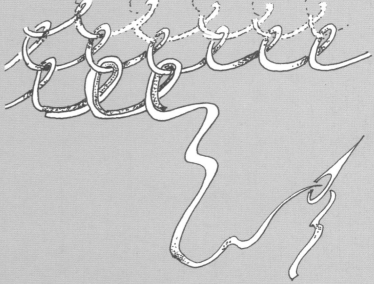

Figure 13

STITCH TENSION

Vary the tension from loose to tight to create very different looks in the body of a looped piece.

LOOSE LOOPING

Loose looping has an airy, netted look with more visible loops. This kind of looping works well as surface design component on top of other materials, since they can be seen through the stitching (figure 14).

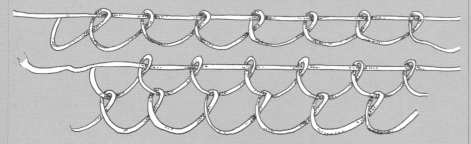

Figure 14

If you use loose looping over a mold, you'll have more control over the path and pattern of the looping. You'll also be able to expose areas of interest on the mold.

If you use a temporary mold with circular looping to create a pouchlike piece, you have the option of placing decorative items back in the pouch. Loose flat looping is also very effective.

TIGHT LOOPING

To create tight looping, simply pull in the stitches more, making sure to do it consistently (figure 15). This technique works well for circular or flat looping. You must use a needle to do this kind of looping, even when using wire. Be sure that the loops you make are large enough to accommodate the needle.

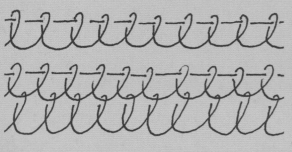

Figure 15

DECREASING CIRCULAR LOOPING

To taper and eventually close off the bottom of a circular looped piece, you must gradually decrease the size of the looping as you're nearing its end.

After you add your last regular row of looping (figure 16), stitch through every other loop on this row to form the next row, drawing the loops closer together and reducing the size of the piece (figure 17). As you do this, also decrease the loop size slightly to account for the larger space left by skipping a loop.

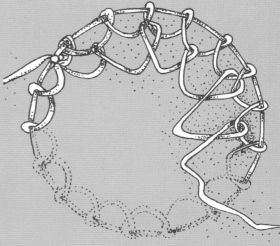

Figure 16

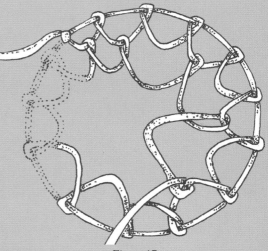

Figure 17

DECREASING FLAT LOOPING

To decrease flat looping, simply skip the last loop on one end of the stitching or on both ends, depending on the shape you wish to create. Turn the piece around before looping across to the other side.

Here are some variations on this idea:

If you consistently eliminate stitches on one end, the results will be a triangular piece with a straight vertical side (figure 18).

Figure 18

If you consistently drop a stitch on both sides, you'll end up with a shape that resembles an equilateral triangle (figure 19).

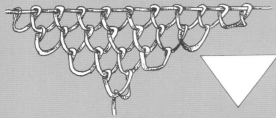

Figure 19

If you want to create an elongated triangle, keep the count of the loops the same for several rows before you begin decreasing them by one on each end (figure 20).

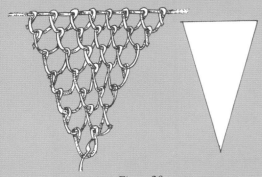

Figure 20

ENDING TECHNIQUES FOR LOOPING

When you come to the end of a looped piece and are ready to stop the process, you have two options. You can either hide the material in the looping or leave a tail hanging and use it as fringe.

ENDING CIRCULAR LOOPING

End the looping process on a circular piece when the diameter of the circle is almost closed. At this point, gather the last few loops together by stitching through each, and pull gently to close the circle (figure 21).

To hide the end of the material, reverse your stitching, following the looping pattern of the previous row. Cut the end of the material carefully (figure 22).

If you want to leave a tail to use for fringe, tie a small knot around the final loops, and bring the material out of the bottom of the piece (figure 23).

ENDING FLAT LOOPING

When you work with flat looping and reach the final loop, you can hide the end in the previous rows (figure 24). If you're working with a decreased piece, you can knot the material on the last row and use it as fringe for adding beads or trinkets (figure 25).

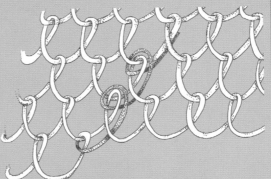

Figure 24

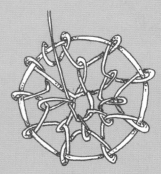

Figure 21

Figure 22

Figure 23

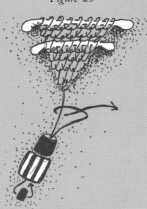

Figure 25

This simple pouch is a great way to learn the basics of circular looping. It is made with a temporary mold that, once removed, allows you to place pebbles, tumbled glass, or other found treasures inside before closing it with a drawstring.

■ MATERIALS

4-ply waxed linen in one color, 30 feet (weaver and neck cord)

Rocks, tumbled glass, or found objects (pouch contents)

Variety of medium-size beads (embellishment)

18-gauge silver wire, 16 inches (dangles)

■ TOOLS

Scissors

Measuring tape

Tapestry needle

Cardboard paper roll or other round temporary mold

Wire cutters

Hammer

Anvil

Needle-nose pliers

■ TECHNIQUES

Temporary mold (see page 86)

Circular looping (see page 87)

Splicing fiber (see page 89)

Loose looping (see page 90)

Decreasing circular looping (see page 90)

Ending techniques (see page 91)

Forging metals (see page 27)

Finishes (see page 20)

■ INSTRUCTIONS

1. Cut three 10-foot lengths of 4-ply waxed linen. Tie one of these lengths around the temporary mold, leaving a 4-inch tail. (This band will form the top opening of the pouch.)

2. Thread the long end of the linen with a tapestry needle, and begin looping around the band with 34 to 44 loose loops spaced about 1/8 inch apart around the circumference of the mold (photo 1).

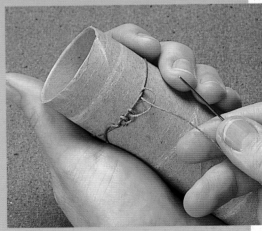

Photo 1

3. Continue to loop, maintaining a consistent size and tension against the mold. When you have completed several rows, thread the tail back through them. Cut off the end and hide it inside the pouch.

4. Splice in a new 10-foot piece of linen (photo 2).

Photo 2

5. When you have completed approximately 18 rows, slide the woven piece to the bottom of the mold to close the bottom of it (photo 3).

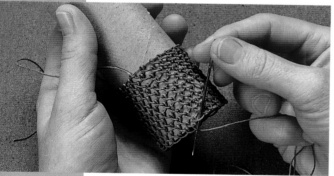

Photo 3

6. Finish the base of the pouch by decreasing the looping (photo 4). Pull the last loops together to close the piece, and thread the tail back through the rows as you did in step 3.

Photo 4

7. Cut two 12-inch lengths of waxed linen to make a drawstring. Thread a tapestry needle with one of the lengths. Stitch in and out of the second row of loops around the top of the pouch, leaving one loop blank between each stitch. Use the second length of linen to thread the fourth row on the opposite side (figure 1).

8. Make a loose half-hitch neck cord from the 4-ply waxed linen, and use a tapestry needle to attach it to the pouch.

9. Use the wire cutters to cut four pieces of 18-gauge silver wire, each 4 inches long. Forge the end of each to create a paddle shape. Loop and twist the other end to create silver dangles (figure 2).

10. Thread beads onto the ends of the drawstrings (figure 3). Then, on the ends of each thread, tie on a silver dangle using a square knot.

11. Place objects inside the pouch before pulling the drawstring to close it.

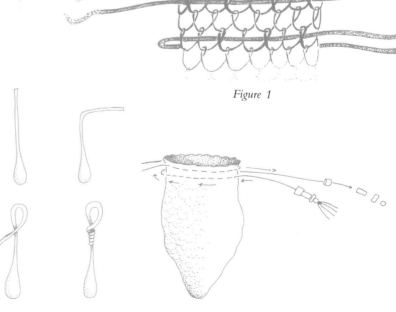

Figure 1

Figure 2

Figure 3

WILD CHERRY NECKLACE

IN THIS PROJECT, YOU'LL LOOP ONTO A PERMANENT MOLD THAT BECOMES AN INTEGRAL PART OF THE JEWELRY. ADDING RAFFIA TO WAXED LINEN CREATES A NICE CONTRAST BETWEEN MATERIALS, AND THE RICH COLOR OF THE BARK SHOWS OFF THE LOOPING.

Techniques

Permanent mold (see page 86)

Circular looping (see page 87)

Adding materials (see page 88)

Ending looping (see page 91)

Finishes (see page 20)

Materials

Wild cherry bark, about 3 x 3 inches (mold)

4-ply waxed linen, 25 feet (weaver and neck cord)

Raffia, 5 feet (added element)

Small beads (embellishment)

Tools

Clothespin

Measuring tape

Handheld drill

1/16-inch drill bit

Scissors

Tapestry needle

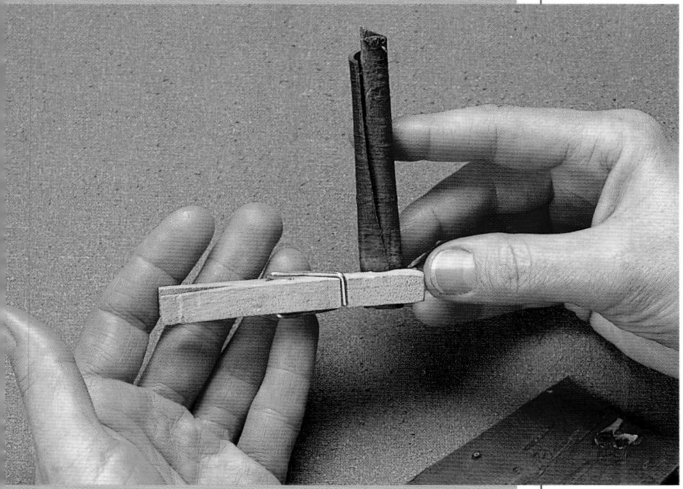

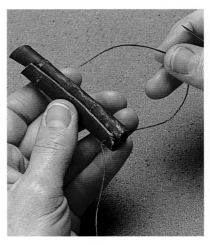

Photo 1

Instructions

1. Prepare the wild cherry bark by soaking it in warm water for half an hour. While still wet, roll or fold it into a somewhat circular overlapping shape to form the permanent mold. Secure the bottom with a clothespin and allow it to dry (photo 1).

2. After it dries, drill a hole about 1/4 inch up from the bottom of the mold. Since the bark is somewhat flattened at this end, it makes this task easier. This hole is the starting point for the looping (figure 1).

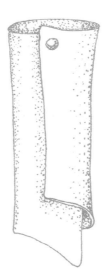

Figure 1

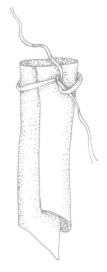

Photo 2

3. Use scissors to cut off a 10-foot length of the waxed linen, and thread one end of it through the hole from the back of the bark to the front, leaving a 4-inch tail (photo 2). Carry the long end of the thread around the bark, returning to the front of the hole. Thread the long piece through the hole from the back or front, and tie the two ends together, making a complete circle (figure 2).

Figure 2

Allow the tail to hang, and thread the tapestry needle with the longer length of thread in preparation for looping (figure 3).

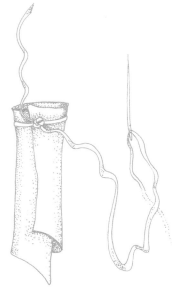

Figure 3

4. Loop approximately 15 to 20 loops around the tied thread, depending on the size of the frame (figure 4). Begin with fairly tight and evenly spaced loops.

5. Stitch three to six rows of looping to form the border of the design before you start adding the raffia. Pause mid-row on the back of the piece to begin this process.

6. Tuck the end of the raffia into the looping (photo 3), and add it in for about 16 rows or enough to cover the majority of the mold. Leave the top of the bark exposed.

7. After the raffia has been added, repeat step 4 to create the top border.

8. Hide the end of the thread by running the needle between the bark and looping until you reach the drilled hole. Tie the thread to the 4-inch tail. Add beads to the hanging threads (figure 5), and tie knots near the ends to hold the beads. Trim the threads and fray them.

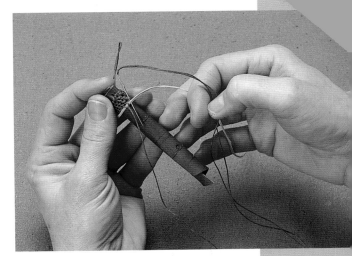

Photo 3

9. Make a plain neck cord of waxed linen. Use a tapestry needle to attach it to the top of the piece.

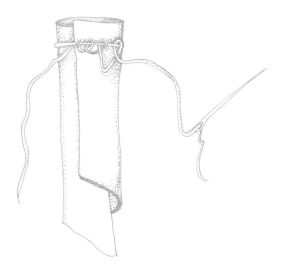

Figure 4

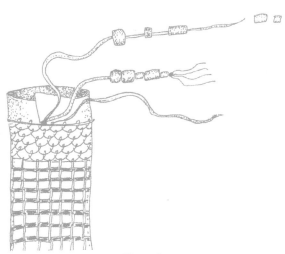

Figure 5

THIS PROJECT USES CIRCULAR LOOPING, SHOWING YOU ONCE AGAIN THE VARIED EFFECTS OF USING DIFFERENT MATERIALS FOR LOOPING. ON THE PERMANENT MOLD, YOU'LL LEAVE OPEN AREAS IN RESPONSE TO THE IRREGULAR SHAPE OF THIS FOUND OBJECT. YOU'LL ALSO LEARN HOW TO ANCHOR THE WIRE TO THE MOLD WITHOUT THREADING IT THROUGH A HOLE.

■ MATERIALS

Found object such as flat stone, beach glass, wood, bone, or ceramic shard (mold)

24- or 26-gauge silver or copper wire, 15 to 25 feet (weaver)

4-ply waxed linen, 10 feet (neck cord)

■ TOOLS

Wire cutters

Measuring tape

Scissors

■ TECHNIQUES

Permanent mold (see page 86)

Circular looping (see page 87)

Loose looping (see page 90)

■ INSTRUCTIONS

1. Select a found object with an interesting shape to use as a mold (photo 1). Decide on the orientation of the piece, since it will eventually hang on the end of the neck cord.

Photo 1

2. Use wire cutters to cut a 5-foot length of wire. In preparation for circular looping, wrap the wire around the top of the mold and secure the wire by wrapping it on itself (figure 1).

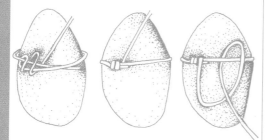

Figure 1

3. Begin looping the wire by hand. Since this wire is rigid, you will not need a tapestry needle. Space the loops loosely and evenly, about 1/8 inch apart. It will be a challenge to work with the wire, but be patient. Pay attention to the tension and try to keep it consistent (photo 2).

4. Continue looping rows as you move toward the bottom of the piece. If you want to create an open area in the looping, move from a loop in a row and skip several loops to connect the wire further along (figure 2). By doing this, you'll expose an area of the mold (photo 3).

5. Once the open area has been established, loop onto the extended wire (figure 3).

6. Bury the end of the wire in the looping after closing the circle. Thread it back up through the looping, following the same pattern.

7. Finish the piece by loosely knotting the waxed linen neck cord, and attaching it to either side around the wire looping.

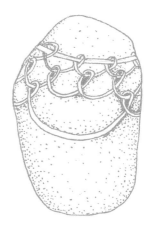

Figure 2

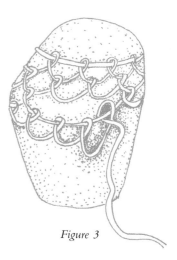

Figure 3

Photo 2

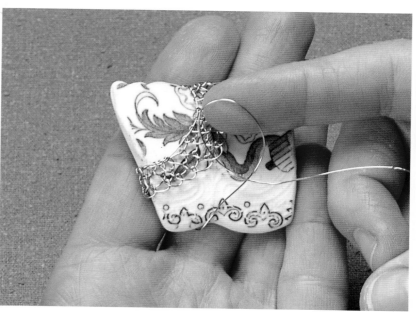

Photo 3

LOOPED LINEN NECKLACE

THIS IS THE MOST CHALLENGING OF THE LOOPING PROJECTS BECAUSE IT REQUIRES YOU TO BUILD THE CIRCULAR LOOPING ON A FRAME MADE OF WIRES. THE TIGHT LOOPING HOLDS THE SHAPE OF THE WIRE STRUCTURE.

Forging metals (see page 27)

Permanent mold (see page 86)

Circular looping (see page 87)

Splicing (see page 89)

Tight looping (see page 90)

Adding materials (see page 88)

Finishes (see page 20)

■ MATERIALS

18-gauge silver wire, 20 inches (frame)

4-ply waxed linen, 30 feet (weaver and neck cord)

■ TOOLS

Wire cutters

Measuring tape

Safety glasses

Hammer

Anvil

Scissors

Tapestry needle

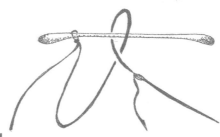

Photo 1

■ INSTRUCTIONS

1. Cut the following pieces from the silver wire: four 2½-inch lengths (rim pieces and additional front and back pieces), two 3½-inch lengths (vertical side pieces), and one 3½-inch length (base wire piece).

2. Wearing safety glasses, forge the ends of the wires until they're flat.

3. Use scissors to cut a 5-foot length of waxed linen.

4. To set up the looping, tie the end of the linen onto one of the 2½-inch silver pieces about ½ inch from one end. Leave a 4-inch tail that will eventually be used to make fringe (figure 1). This top wire will form the rim on the front of the necklace.

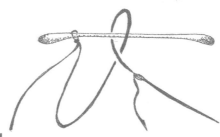

Figure 1

5. Thread the longer end of the linen onto the tapestry needle and begin looping across the piece, forming approximately 20 tight loops (photo 1). Keep the loops and tension consistent, allowing enough slack to insert the tapestry needle when you add the next row.

6. Pick up a second 2½-inch silver wire piece to use as the back rim. Secure it to the front rim piece with two loops, knotting tightly around the connection, and leaving the forged paddles exposed (photo 2).

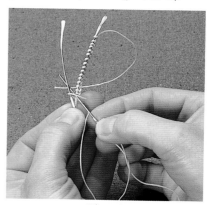

Photo 2

7. Continue looping around the top of the pouch on the back rim (photo 3), adding the same number of loops you added to the first. After you're done, tie together the two pieces of silver with the looping linen and tail.

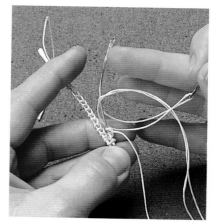

Photo 3

8. Add a second row of looping to the first, all the way around. When you've completed this row, add one 3½-inch-long silver vertical piece. Anchor it by looping around it before you stitch back through a couple of times to secure it (photo 4). Continue looping onto the back rim piece until you reach the other side, and add the second 3½-inch-long silver piece.

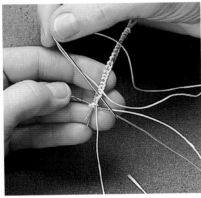

Photo 4

9. Loop two more complete rows of the same count all the way around the piece, looping once around the vertical pieces to secure them in the looping. Maintain the same loop count to keep the pouch from pulling in and losing its shape (figure 2).

Figure 2

10. Loop in one of the two remaining 2½-inch silver pieces as a decorative element that reflects the top rim piece (photo 5). When you turn the pouch, loop in the other 2½-inch silver piece on the other side.

Photo 5

11. Continue to loop the pouch, totaling 24 to 28 rows. Keep in mind that the wire paddles should stay exposed.

12. As you begin to run out of linen, splice in a 5-foot length. It should be enough to finish the body of the piece.

13. Bend the remaining 3½-inch silver piece to form the base insert (figure 3). The center horizontal section of this bent wire should be about ½ inch wide. The two legs should

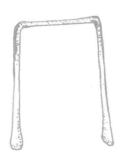

Figure 3

be about 1½ inches each so that the center section fits between the vertical pieces.

14. Close the bottom of the piece by looping around the inserted wire with the thread (figure 4). Use a whipstitch to

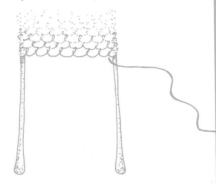

Figure 4

gather the two sides of looping and the inserted wire to tightly close the bottom (photo 6).

15. Anchor the end of the thread by stitching it back into the body of the piece, following the looping to the top rim that has no hanging tail of thread. Use a half-hitch knot to secure the thread to the top corner. Cut the end of the thread to match the tail on the other side so you have tails for making fringe on both sides.

Photo 6

16. Cut off about 10 feet of waxed linen and make a tight half-hitch neck cord from it. Tie the ends of the cord to two of the top silver pieces, leaving ½ inch tails to add more fringe.

In this project, you'll use flat looping to create a delicate and open design punctuated by graduated silver ribs. This necklace pendant is simple to make, but the results are quite elegant.

■ MATERIALS

18-gauge silver wire, 2 feet (ribs)

24- or 26-gauge silver wire, 20 feet (weaver)

Beads or jewelry trinket (embellishment)

2 medium-size jump rings (connections)

18- or 24-inch-long commercially made silver neck chain (finish)

■ TOOLS

Wire cutters

Measuring tape

Safety glasses

Hammer

Anvil

2 pairs of needle-nose pliers

■ TECHNIQUES

Forging metals (see page 27)

Flat looping (see page 88)

Loose looping (see page 90)

Adding materials (see page 88)

Decreasing flat looping (see page 91)

■ INSTRUCTIONS

1. Cut a piece of 18-gauge silver wire that's about 3 inches long. Cut six more pieces, reducing the size of each by about 1/2 inch, until the smallest piece is about 1/2 inch.

2. Wearing safety glasses, forge both ends of each of the wires. Lay them out in a vertical ascending pattern.

3. Cut off 5 feet of the smaller gauge silver wire. To attach the end of the wire, wrap the left side of the longest forged silver piece, tucking the tail beneath the wrapping (figure 1). Wrap it six to 10 times, covering the tail (figure 2).

Figure 1

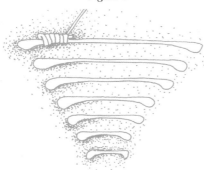

Figure 2

4. Loop loosely across this top rib at least 20 times before reaching the opposite side (photo 1). When you end the looping, wrap the right end as you did the beginning of the left. Carry the wire to the next row to begin looping.

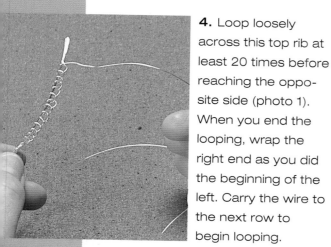

Photo 1

5. Turn the piece to the other side and continue with flat looping on the established row (photo 2). Loop a total of two to three rows before adding in the next piece of forged 18-gauge wire (photo 3).

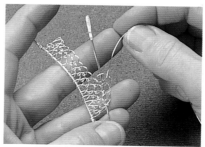

Photo 2

Photo 3

6. Each time you add in a smaller piece, decrease the looping on each end by one.

7. Continue to loop two to three rows between the ribs, adding in the next graduated size (photo 4). Keep decreasing the stitching on the rows to create the triangular effect.

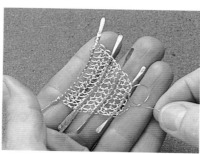

Photo 4

8. Once you've added all the pieces, decrease the looping to form a point at the end. Bring the end of the wire out the bottom and add a trinket or beads for embellishment.

9. Use two pairs of pliers to open one of the jump rings. To do this, grasp the ring on either side of the split and twist gently in opposite directions so it doesn't get distorted. Insert the ring into the top of the piece between the loops, about 3/4 inch from one end (photo 5). Close the ring the same way you opened it, so you don't distort it. Insert the second ring on the other side, the same distance from the end (figure 3).

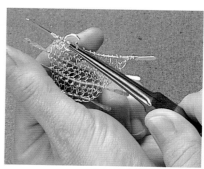

Photo 5

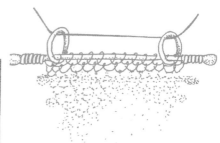

Figure 3

10. Thread the neck chain through the two jump rings.

VARIATIONS

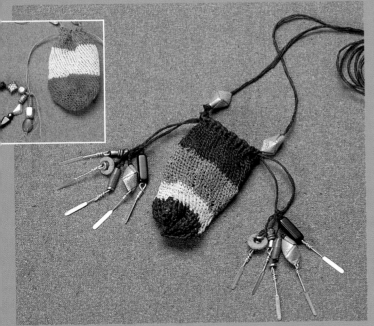

LOOPED POUCH NECKLACES

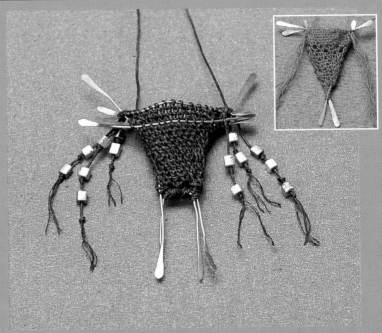

LOOPED LINEN NECKLACES

NECKLACES LOOPED OVER PERMANENT MOLD

SILVER FISHBONE NECKLACES

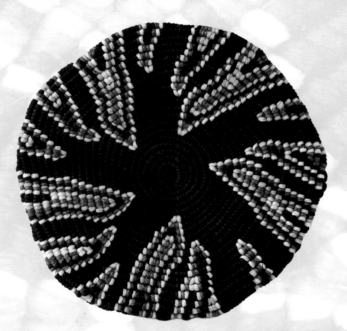

KNOTTIN

Contemporary basket makers often use the traditional medium of knotting in new and interesting ways. A multitude of styles and interpretations of this technique are used to make fascinating pieces, such as sculptural vessel forms. These ideas translate well into jewelry made of both soft fiber and metal. In this section, you'll use knotting to create flat jewelry pieces and dimensional pouches.

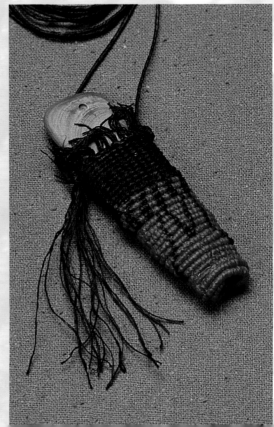

KNOTTING

■ BASIC KNOTTING IS DONE WITH A SERIES OF HALF-HITCH KNOTS COMMONLY USED IN MACRAMÉ OR CHINESE KNOTTING. THE MECHANICS OF KNOTTING INVOLVE TWO BASIC ELEMENTS: THE CORE, OR THE MATERIAL THAT RUNS CONTINUOUSLY THROUGHOUT THE STRUCTURE, AND THE BINDER, OR THE FLEXIBLE MATERIAL THAT'S KNOTTED OVER THE CORE.

WAXED LINEN, EMBROIDERY FLOSS, AND WIRES ARE USED FOR THE PROJECTS. IF WAXED LINEN IS USED, 6- OR 7-PLY THREADS ARE USED FOR THE CORE AND BINDERS ARE MADE OF 3- OR 4-PLY THREAD. WHEN WIRE IS USED, THE CORE IS MADE OF 18-GAUGE MATERIAL AND BINDERS ARE 24-GAUGE OR SMALLER.

ATTACHING BINDER THREADS TO THE CORE

For knotted projects made with a core of a consistent diameter, or for projects in which the knotting is done on a core around a mold with a consistent diameter, you can calculate the length of the binders needed to cover the core. To do this, multiply 10 by the length of the area you'll cover on the mold, the radius of the projected circular piece, or the height of a dimensional piece. If you want more creative leeway concerning the finished size, multiply by 15.

For example, if you want to cover 3 inches of a straight dowel, multiply three by 10, and cut 30-inch binder threads. If you want to make a flat circular piece that is 6 inches in diameter, multiply the radius of 3 inches by 10 as well. When the threads are folded in half and knotted to the core, you'll be working with individual strands half this length.

If you happen to be knotting onto a permanent mold that fluctuates in diameter, you can reduce the number of binder threads as you work (see page 113).

For each project, you'll use binders of different lengths and numbers. For example, if you're beginning a small circular piece, you'll use only a few binder threads to begin covering the core that forms its center. The following explains how to attach the binder threads so you can begin the knotting process.

1. Horizontally position the end of the long core material on your work surface. Cut several binder threads to the appropriate lengths and loop them in half.

2. Use a Lark's head knot to attach the center of the looped binder to the core (figure 1). To do this, bend the loop over the front of the core, and thread the two ends of the binder threads through it. Pull the ends of the binders to secure the knot around the core.

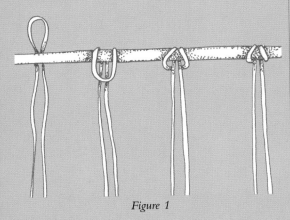

Figure 1

3. Attach the remaining binder threads side by side to the core.

BEGINNING TO KNOT

All of the knotting projects in this book are made with the same kind of simple half-hitch knot. After you've attached the binder threads, you're ready to begin knotting the binder material onto the core, using a series of these knots. Remember, you'll work with only one strand of the binder at a time.

1. Loop the binder thread underneath and over the core (figure 2).

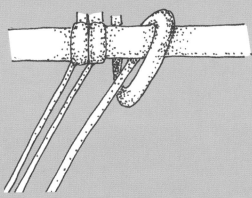

Figure 2

2. Pull the half-hitch knot to secure it on the core (figure 3).

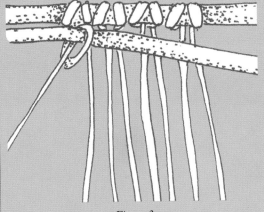

Figure 3

CIRCULAR KNOTTING

Circular knotting is continuous. You'll fan the binder threads in a circular configuration as you work, knotting them to the core and pulling it around itself to form a spiral-shaped form.

MAKING THE CORE CIRCLE OR BASE

This initial work results in the center of a flat circular piece or the base of a dimensional piece.

1. Before you begin circular knotting, add the binder threads to the core, leaving a tail that's 4 inches or shorter on one end (figure 4). If the core is made of thread with multiple plies, reduce the bulk of the tail by cutting out about half of the strands. This step is important later when you need to conceal the tail in the knotting. If the core is made of a solid material, such as wire, trim the material at an angle.

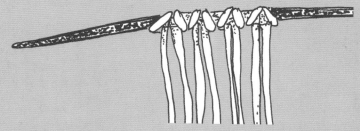

Figure 4

2. To begin the circular core or base, curl the long length of the core over the tail, making a circular shape. Allow the binder threads to fan out from the core. Begin attaching the core to itself by half-hitching one strand around it. Continue to knot around the core, using one strand at a time in sequence. Incorporate the tail into the knotting as you progress around the piece (figure 5).

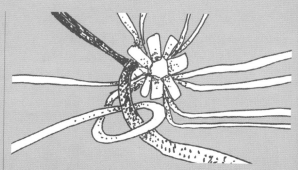

Figure 5

CUPPED CIRCULAR

If you continue to knot from the base and don't add in extra binder threads, the shape will gradually cup up from the core. This technique is used to make dimensional pouches and other shaped pieces.

FLAT CIRCULAR AND ADDING IN BINDER THREADS

If you want to make a flat circular shape, you'll add extra binder threads to the core as you work, allowing it to flatten out and grow in diameter. Apply this same method to add in binder threads to any piece.

1. Use the same Lark's head knot to add extra threads to the progressing half-hitched core (figure 6). To keep the piece totally flat, add in enough binders to keep the core covered as you work. You can also use these threads to add new colors.

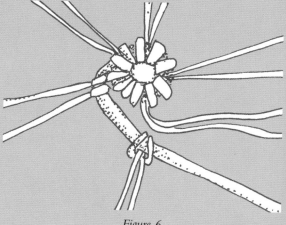

Figure 6

2. Continue this process as you knot around the piece, adding binders as needed. If the binders you're using aren't completely covering the core, it's time to add a new thread (figure 7).

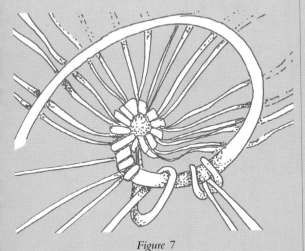

Figure 7

OPEN-ENDED CIRCULAR

To knot on a permanent mold that you want to leave partially exposed, you can create an opening at the top of the knotting. Then you'll knot around the mold from the top down.

1. In the usual fashion, begin by attaching the binders to the core thread with Lark's head knots. Instead of pulling the binders tightly to make a spiral, leave a circular opening that fits around the particular mold you're using, then use a half-hitch knot to begin your work (figure 8).

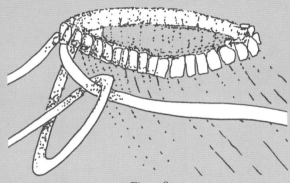

Figure 8

2. If you're covering an entire mold, do so by knotting until the piece is covered. If the mold is uneven, you may have to reduce the number of binder threads or add in binder threads as you work to accommodate the shape.

REDUCING BINDER THREADS

You can decrease the size of a project as you knot it by reducing the number of binder threads. This loss of threads will pull in the body of the piece as you keep the core covered. As you work with less binder threads, you'll be knotting less and the size of the piece will decrease.

1. Bend the thread you wish to eliminate to the back side of the core in the direction of the knotting, in preparation for incorporating it into the knotting along the core (figure 9).

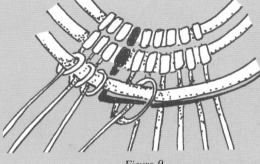

Figure 9

2. As you knot, lay the binder thread on the core and half-hitch it with the next binder thread. As you continue knotting, you'll cover this thread with the active binders (figure 10). Continue to knot, covering the thread and core together with several more half-hitch knots, then cut off the tail of the binder you're eliminating.

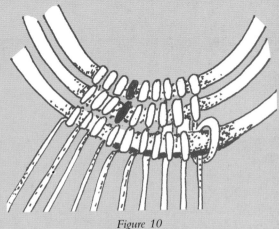

Figure 10

FLAT KNOTTING

Like circular knotting, flat knotting is also composed of a series of half-hitch knots, binding the core material onto itself to make linear coils. You'll attach the initial binders with Lark's head knots and calculate the length of the binders in the same way as you did a circular binder.

To make flat pieces, you can knot together separate pieces of cut core, or knot a continuous core, depending on the look you want. You'll use consecutive rows of knotting to connect the core or core pieces as described below.

FLAT KNOTTING WITH SEPARATE CORE PIECES

Cut pieces of core material and lay them out lengthwise. Attach binder threads to the top core piece with Lark's head knots, making certain you cover the core. Once the binder threads are in place, place the next piece of core material directly underneath the original one. Use the binder threads and half-hitch knots to connect the second row. When you reach the end of a row, reverse the direction of the knotting and go back across the core (figure 11). Continue in this fashion to add rows (figure 12).

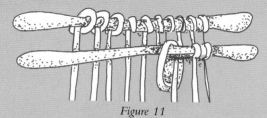

Figure 11

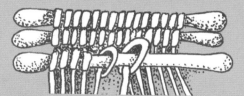

Figure 12

When you create flat knotting from the front, the back side will look different because the binder threads form a vertical stitch, while the front appears clean and coiled (figure 13).

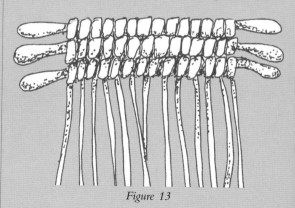

Figure 13

FLAT KNOTTING WITH CONTINUOUS CORE MATERIAL

The second method of flat knotting uses one long continuous core. Once you have placed the binder threads on the end of the core material, stopping when you've established the width of the piece, simply bend the core and use half-hitch knots to begin attaching the core onto itself (figure 14).

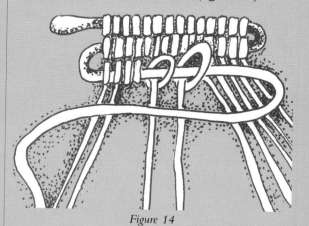

Figure 14

ENDING KNOTTING

When the knotting is complete, you'll have to finish the core of the piece. One option is to make the binder threads into fringe as shown in all of the knotting projects that follow this section.

CIRCULAR

To finish circular knotting, whether flat or dimensional, eliminate the core by anchoring it to the inside or back of the piece. If the piece is round and flat, tuck the core on the back (figure 15). Find the binder thread closest to the end of the knotting, and use a tapestry needle to stitch the core to the back. Be careful not to stitch through to the front, and pull the core tightly. If it's a dimensional piece with sides, such as a pouch, or if the knotting is done over a mold, simply tuck the core material to the inside and use the closest binder thread to anchor it with a stitch or two.

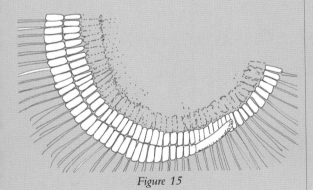

Figure 15

FLAT

When knotting a flat piece, you can stop the project at the end of a row by simply cutting the continuous core. If you're working with separate core pieces, just stop adding more of them.

BINDER THREADS AS FRINGE

You can cut binder threads to any length you wish and use them as decorative fringe (figure 16). If you're working with wire binders, burn the ends to create a finished look (figure 17).

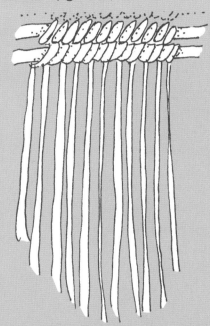

Figure 16

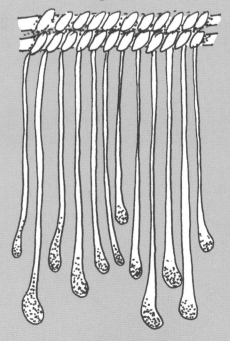

Figure 17

This necklace shows how you can integrate knotting and an interesting piece of driftwood. Silver beads incorporated into the black waxed linen core add striking contrast. Since each piece of wood is unique, find one that suits the character of your design.

■ MATERIALS

6- or 7-ply black waxed linen, 10 feet (core and neck cord)

4-ply black waxed linen, 20 feet (binder)

8 to 10 small silver beads (embellishment)

2 accent silver beads, 2 round black beads, and 2 small copper beads (embellishment)

■ TOOLS

Handheld drill

$1/16$-inch bit

Scissors

Measuring tape

■ TECHNIQUES

Attaching binder threads to the core (see page 110)

Circular knotting/open-ended (see page 113)

Adding in binder threads (see page 112)

Reducing binder threads (see page 113)

Ending circular core (see page 115)

Ending knotting/binders as fringe (see page 115)

■ INSTRUCTIONS

1. Study the piece of wood and decide how you want it to hang on the necklace. Then decide which end you'd like to begin the knotting on, and drill a hole close to this end (photo 1).

Photo 2

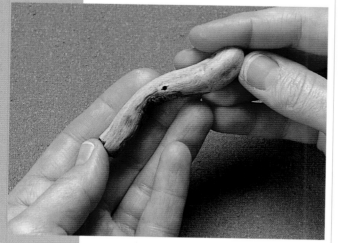

Photo 1

2. Cut a 5-foot length of the 6- or 7-ply waxed linen. Thread the end of it through the hole and tie it to the wood to anchor it, leaving a tail approximately 4 inches long. The other long piece of linen is the core.

3. Cut binder threads from the 4-ply waxed linen to cover a 2-inch-long area, thus each is 20 inches long. Cut about 12 binder threads of this length or as many needed to cover a portion of the core so it fits around the wood. Attach them to the core with Lark's head knots (photo 2). Circle the piece of wood with the covered core.

4. Use the binders to half-hitch the second row of core to the first.

5. Continue to knot, adding more binder threads if the diameter of the wood increases in some spots, and reducing the number if the wood decreases in other places.

6. Add a silver bead to the core in place of a binder thread (photo 3). To create a diagonal pattern of beads, add beads in a staggered pattern (photo 4).

7. Continue to knot until you've covered about 2 inches of the piece. End the knotting by cut-

Photo 3

Photo 4

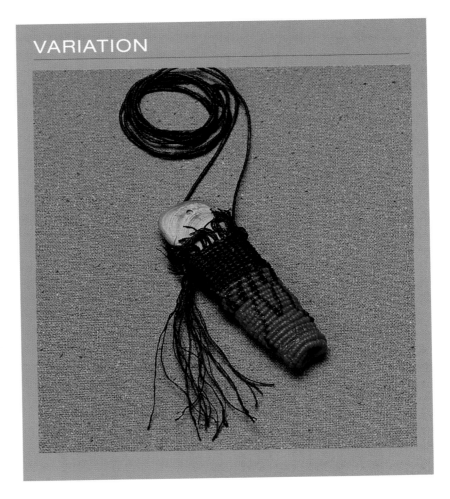

Figure 1

ting the core to about ½ inch long and tucking it underneath the knotting so it is secure.

8. Trim the binder threads so they form a fringe.

9. Cut a neck cord from black waxed linen in a length of your choice and add the embellishment beads to it.

10. Drill two new holes on either end of the wood. Thread and tie the ends of the cord through each hole (figure 1). The beads on the neck cord will rest on top of the wood.

VARIATION

VESSEL-SHAPED KNOTTED PIN

ENCASE A FOUND OBJECT
IN KNOTTING TO CREATE A
BEAUTIFULLY SHAPED PIECE.
YOUR BIGGEST CHALLENGE
WILL BE ADDING AND
DECREASING THE KNOTTING
TO CONFORM TO THE
OBJECT'S SHAPE.

■ INSTRUCTIONS

1. Measure the length of the mold you're covering, and multiply that number by 10 to determine the length of the binder threads.

2. Using this measurement, cut approximately 12 lengths of 4-ply waxed linen for the binders. Find the centers of the binders and attach four of them to the 6- or 7-ply waxed linen core.

3. Begin knotting to form the circular base. Hold the mold in place as you knot. If needed, use a bit of instant-bonding glue to secure the mold to the knotting at this point.

4. Follow the shape of your mold while adding in new binder threads of embroidery floss to create patterns (photo 1).

5. Conform to the shape, decreasing or loosening the binders as needed. Complete one-half to three-quarters of the total project, then stop to add the stickpin.

6. Put a drop of glue on the flat part of the head, and place it firmly on the mold where you want the head of the pin to exit the knotting (figure 1). Continue knotting, covering the head of the pin completely (figure 2).

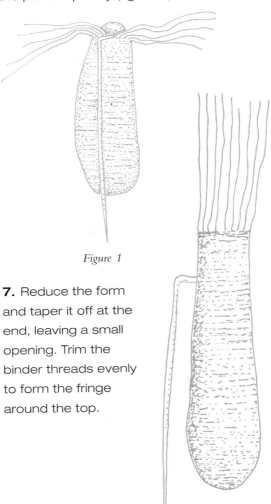

Figure 1

7. Reduce the form and taper it off at the end, leaving a small opening. Trim the binder threads evenly to form the fringe around the top.

Figure 2

Photo 1

■ TECHNIQUES

Attaching binder threads to the core (see page 110)

Making the core circle or base (see page 112)

Circular knotting, cupped (see page 112)

Ending circular core (see page 115)

Ending knotting/binders as fringe (see page 115)

■ MATERIALS

Tapered found object such as a stick or rock

4-ply waxed linen, 25 feet (main binder color)

6- or 7-ply waxed linen, 8 feet (core)

3 embroidery floss colors, 7 yards each (accent binder colors)

2 metallic embroidery floss colors, 7 yards each (accent binder colors)

Stickpin with round head (finish)

■ TOOLS

Measuring tape

Scissors

Instant-bonding glue

CONE-SHAPED POUCH PIN

A CARDBOARD CONE USED AS A TEMPORARY MOLD IS THE KEY TO MAKING THIS INTERESTING PIN. YOU'LL ADD MORE BINDER THREADS TO INCREASE THE SIZE OF THE SHAPE AS YOU WORK, CREATING A SPIRALING PATTERN.

■ INSTRUCTIONS

1. Cut 12 pieces from the 4-ply waxed linen base binder, each 30 inches long.

2. Attach four of the 12 base color binders to the 9-foot waxed linen core, about 4 inches from one end.

3. Knot the circular base of the piece with the base color binders.

4. Anchor the base to the top of the cardboard cone with a T-pin to hold it in place while you knot. Begin knotting, following the shape of the mold (photo 1).

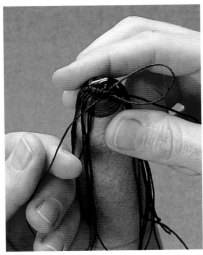

Photo 1

5. Add accent binders as needed to increase the size and also to add color (photo 2).

6. Continue to follow the cone shape, adding in more binder threads as the size increases. Keep the tension snug and don't allow the core to show through.

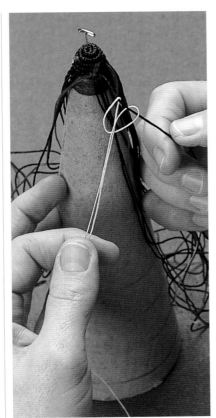

Photo 2

7. Add the stickpin about three-quarters of the way up. Glue the round head to the back wall inside the form to secure it.

8. Continue to knot, embedding the head in the knotting.

9. When you've reached the top of the piece, cut the binder threads to make fringe.

■ TECHNIQUES

Attaching binder threads to the core (see page 110)

Making the core circle or base (see page 112)

Cupped circular knotting (see page 112)

Ending circular core (see page 115)

Ending knotting/binders as fringe (see page 115)

■ MATERIALS

Cone-shaped cardboard mold (available at craft supply stores)

6- or 7-ply black waxed linen, 9 feet (core)

4-ply black waxed linen, 25 to 30 feet (main binder color)

Off-white and dark red waxed linen, 5 yards of each (accent binder colors)

Silver and white metallic embroidery floss colors, 7 yards each (accent binder colors)

■ TOOLS

Scissors

Measuring tape

T-pin

Stickpin with round head

Instant-bonding glue

SUNDIAL PIN

USE A MIXTURE OF WAXED LINEN AND EMBROIDERY FLOSS TO MAKE THIS FLAT, CIRCULAR LAPEL PIN. THE DESIGN GIVES YOU AN OPPORTUNITY TO BLEND VARIOUS SHADES OF EMBROIDERY THREAD TO CREATE A GRADUAL SHIFT IN COLOR. METALLIC THREADS LEND CONTRAST AND A BIT OF SPARKLE.

■ INSTRUCTIONS

1. From each of the 4-ply waxed linen colors, cut a binder that is 20 inches long. Cut 20-inch lengths from the embroidery floss threads as well.

2. Attach four binder threads of waxed linen in the same color to the 7-ply waxed linen core with Lark's head knots (photo 1). These threads will carry through to the next row of core, creating a colorful pattern.

Photo 1

3. Begin the circular knotting, forming the small central core. As the piece grows in diameter, keep it flat by adding new binder threads of various colors (photo 2). Always keep the core covered with threads, and don't leave gaps between them. This addition of threads creates the pattern.

Photo 2

4. When the piece is about 2 1/2 inches in diameter and large enough to cover the bar pin, secure the end of the core to the back by stitching it with binder thread.

5. Trim the binder threads to form a fringe around the piece.

6. Use a tapestry needle and 4-ply waxed linen to sew the bar pin to the back, taking care not to bring the thread through the front of the piece (photo 3).

Photo 3

■ TECHNIQUES

Attaching binder threads to the core (see page 110)

Making the core circle or base (see page 112)

Flat circular knotting and adding binder threads (see page 112)

Ending knotting/circular core (see page 115)

Ending knotting, binder threads as fringe (see page 115)

■ MATERIALS

7-ply neutral waxed linen, 7 feet (core)

4-ply waxed linen in 5 different colors, 5 feet each (binder threads)

3 embroidery floss colors, 7 yards each (binder)

2 metallic embroidery floss colors, 7 yards each (binder)

Bar pin

■ TOOLS

Scissors

Measuring tape

Tapestry needle

KNOTTING RANDOMLY WITH COPPER WIRE CAN PRODUCE A VARIETY OF INTERESTING RESULTS. THIS PIECE, CREATED WITH FLAT KNOTTING OVER SEPARATE CORE PIECES, ILLUSTRATES THE CREATIVE NATURE OF THIS PROCESS.

■ MATERIALS

18-gauge copper wire, 5 feet (core pieces)

24-gauge or smaller copper wire, 60 feet (binder)

Silver neck chain, 18 to 24 inches in length (finishes)

2 copper jump rings (finishes)

■ TOOLS

Wire cutters

Safety glasses

Measuring tape

Torch

2 pairs of needle-nose pliers

■ TECHNIQUES

Finishing the ends of wire (page 28)

Attaching binder threads to the core (see page 110)

Flat knotting with separate core pieces (see page 114)

Ending knotting/binder threads as fringe (see page 115)

1. Wearing safety glasses, cut approximately 15 pieces of the 18-gauge copper wire, each about 3 inches long. Burn the ends of the wires to finish the core pieces.

2. For binders, cut 25 to 30 pieces of the 24-gauge wire, each about 2 feet in length.

3. Attach the binders across one of the 18-gauge core wires, leaving small blank spots on the wire that will leave holes in the knotting (photo 1). Since wire is stiffer than thread, it's sometimes more difficult to keep a consistent shape in the knotting. When you attach a binder, pull it gently with both strands, and smooth out the wires as you add them (photo 2).

Photo 2

4. Add rows of individual core pieces as you knot the piece. Leave open areas between the 18-gauge spokes (photo 3).

6. Use both pairs of needle-nose pliers to attach jump rings to the top length of wire, and thread the necklace chain through the finished piece.

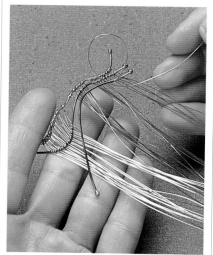

Photo 3

5. After you've added all the spokes, stop the flat knotting. Burn the ends of the wires that form the fringe, then burn portions of the piece's body. To get deeper colors in the copper, heat some areas longer than others (photo 4).

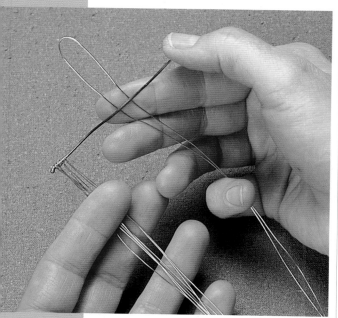

Photo 1

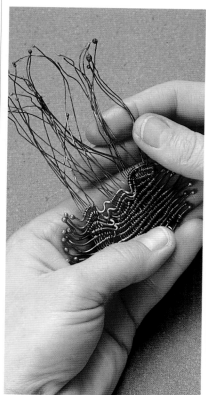

Photo 4

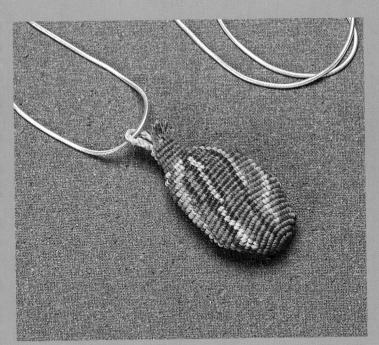

VESSEL-SHAPED NECKLACE

CONE-SHAPED POUCH PIN

SUNDIAL PIN

FREE-FORM KNOTTED NECKLACE

COILING

THIS TECHNIQUE INVOLVES WRAPPING A CORE
WITH A FLEXIBLE BINDING MATERIAL TO CREATE
COILS THAT ARE WOUND TOGETHER TO FORM A
SHAPE, WHETHER CIRCULAR OR OTHERWISE.
USING THIS TECHNIQUE TO MAKE JEWELRY
GIVES YOU ENORMOUS ROOM FOR CREATIVITY
IN MATERIAL, SHAPE, AND DESIGN.

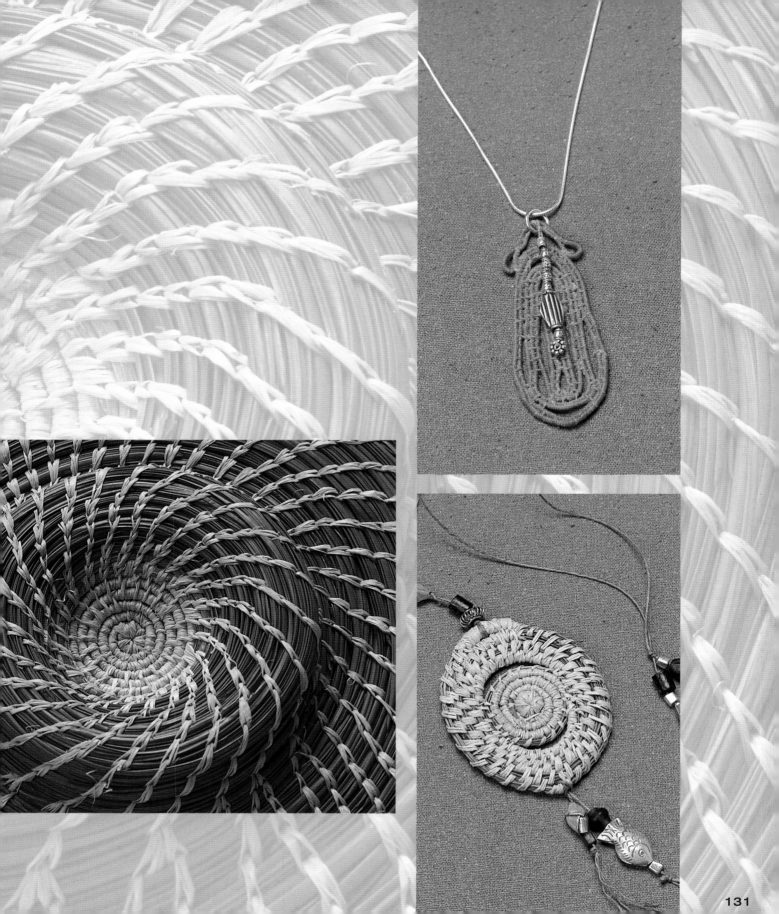

COILING

■ In the projects following this introductory section, the cores are made of either pine needles, wire, or waxed linen. The binder threads are of raffia or waxed linen. All of the projects are coiled flat.

The most traditional form of coiling uses a core of bundled pine needles. You can also use a solid, continuous core of wire or waxed linen. The core must be flexible so that it can be easily curved and shaped. The binder material should be very flexible and strong, and it is normally threaded through a tapestry needle to make it easier to stitch.

BEGINNING A FLAT CIRCULAR PIECE

In this section, you'll learn how to coil a flat circular base from pine needles. This same method can be applied to other materials, but the most traditional form of coiling uses pine needles with a raffia binder. You'll bundle them as you work, forming a multiple-element core. Prepare them ahead by soaking them in warm water.

1. To begin a coiled pine needle project, cut off about a 5-foot length of the raffia. Thin it down by separating it lengthwise, pulling it apart at the thicker end to divide it into thinner strands. Thread it through the tapestry needle and pull it to leave a single working strand (figure 1).

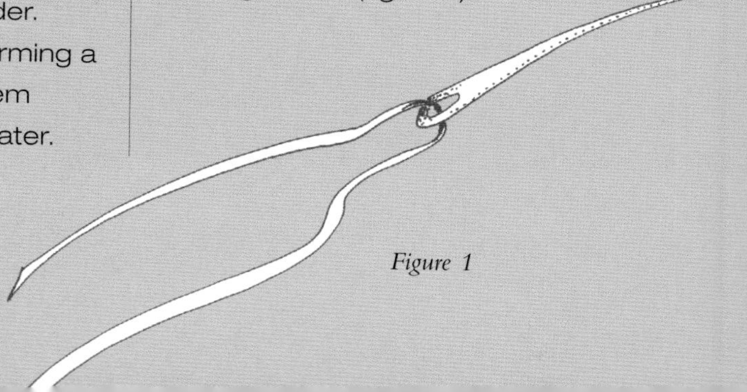

Figure 1

2. Loop two pine needles around your finger in a circle about 1 inch from the heads (figure 2).

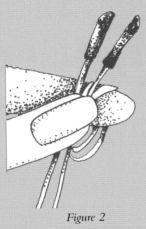

Figure 2

3. Use a double overhand knot to secure the core (figure 3), leaving a tail of about 4 inches (figure 4).

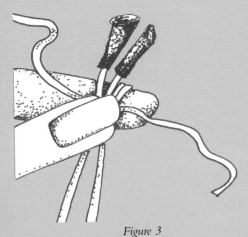

Figure 3

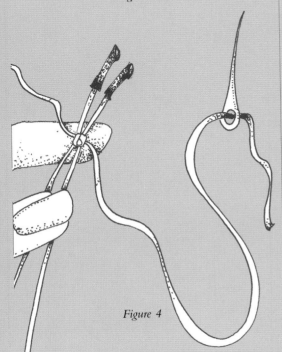

Figure 4

4. Remove the circular piece from your finger, and place the long ends of the needles to the left and the heads of the needles to the right. Hold the circle with your left hand and lay the tail along the length of the needles (figure 5).

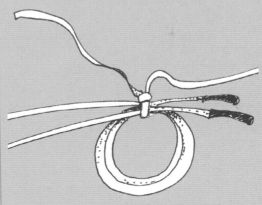

Figure 5

5. Loop the raffia through the hole and cover the tail with several tight wraps to secure the circular core (figure 6). Gently pull the heads and longer ends of the pine needles at the same time to pull in the circle's diameter.

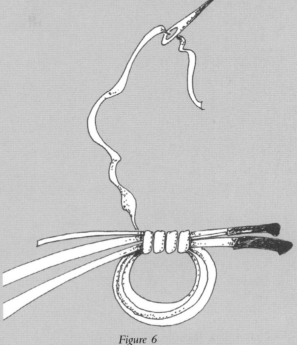

Figure 6

7. Taper the heads of the pine needles, and tuck them into the circular core to finish the first base core (figure 7).

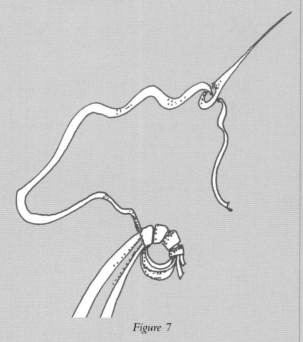

Figure 7

8. Continue stitching to cover the circular core with stitches until you close the circle (figure 8). If a tail is left hanging, trim it, and cover the tapered needles as you close the circle (figure 9).

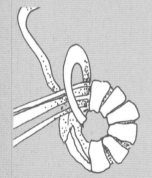

Figure 8

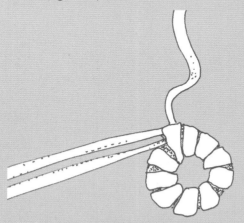

Figure 9

BEGINNING A FLAT OVAL PIECE

This section shows you how to begin an oval shape with coiling. Here we've used a continuous core of waxed linen with a binder of waxed linen, but you can also use other core or binding materials.

1. Cut off about a 5-foot length of 3-ply waxed linen to use as the binder, and thread the needle with it. Cut approximately 5 to 10 feet of 4-ply waxed linen for the core material. Hold the core horizontal with the longer end to the left. Overlap the end of the binder material about 2 inches on the core (figure 10).

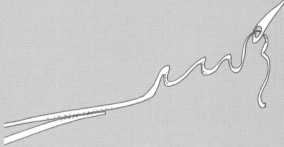

Figure 10

2. Move left as you wrap the core with the binder, covering the tail along with the core (figure 11).

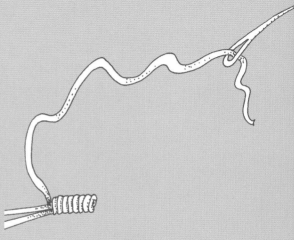

Figure 11

3. Continue to wrap the core until you form one long side of the oval. Add a few extra wraps to cover a bend in the core, and fold the core to the other side (figure 12). Trim the tail of the binder.

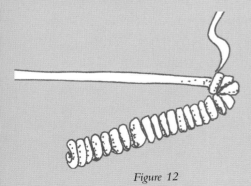

Figure 12

4. Begin to connect the second row of core by wrapping the binder thread around both sides of the core with a lazy stitch (figure 13) before continuing to wrap the uncovered core (figure 14). After adding two more wraps to the uncovered core, repeat this step (figure 15).

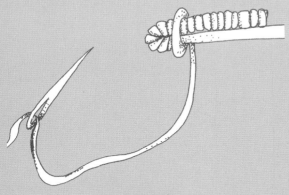

Figure 13

Figure 14

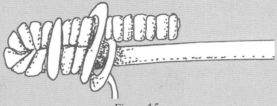

Figure 15

5. Continue with this pattern of wrapping until you close the oval (figure 16).

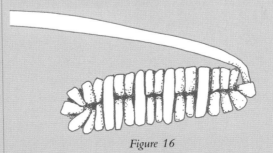

Figure 16

STITCHES USED WITH COILING

Various stitches are used to attach core to core. Descriptions of three common stitches used for this purpose follow. You've already seen the lazy stitch used to make an oval shaped base.

FIGURE-EIGHT STITCH

Begin this stitch with the binding material at the top of the core that you plan to coil. Bind the two cores together by stitching between them to the inside or back (figure 17). Then bring the binder over the front of the bottom core, and stitch between the cores again at the backside and behind the end at the top core (figure 18). Pull the binder taut.

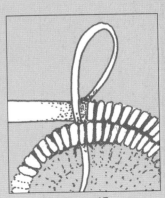

Figure 17

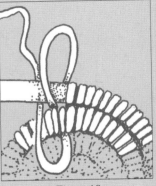

Figure 18

LAZY STITCH

The lazy stitch is used to connect cores. After you make this simple stitch, you can follow it with a series of wraps around the uncovered core before adding another connecting stitch to create continuous coverage (figure 19). If you want to expose the core, as is often done in pine needle coiling, space the stitches apart and then add the next row of stitches as shown (figure 20).

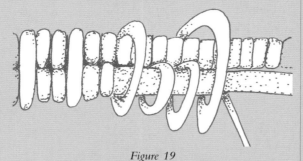

Figure 19

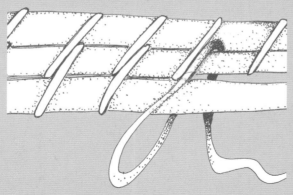

Figure 20

SPLIT STITCH

Begin this stitch after you have completed a row of lazy stitches exposing a multiple-element core. Use the needle to pierce through the center of the binders and core of the previous row. Keep adding sequential stitches to connect the cores (figure 21). Sometimes the pierced binder will split into a V-shape, especially if you're using raffia.

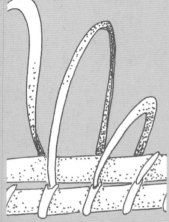

Figure 21

ADDING CORE MATERIAL

If you're using wire as your core material, it's a good idea to make sure that you have enough of a continuous length to complete the whole coiling project, since wire does not splice very easily. However, if needed, it can be done.

To splice wire or waxed linen, cut the end of the material on a diagonal as well as the new material that you're adding (figure 22). Place them together before proceeding.

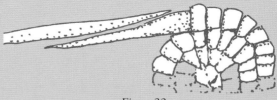

Figure 22

Splicing pine needles is a natural part of the coiling process since the needles are of a limited length. In our example, you began with two intact pine needles with heads that, once removed, form a total of four strands. As you coil the needles around, they will fan out so that the end of each needle runs out at a different point. When one needle runs out, splice in a single strand as shown (figures 23 and 24).

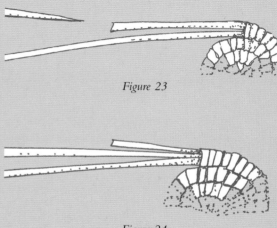

Figure 23

Figure 24

ADDING BINDER MATERIAL

Because binder material is difficult to work with if it is too long, it is often inevitable that you'll run out and need to add more. Adding another binder thread is also a way of changing colors in your design. You can add a new binder thread by incorporating it into the existing core or by tying on a new thread. The tied-on method works well when you are connecting cores with a lazy stitch, which allows part of the core to show.

1. To use the first method, thread the needle onto the tail of the binder. Place a new piece of binder along the core, and use the needle and thread to coil and secure it (figure 25).

2. Trim the old binder after securing the new binder, and thread the needle on the new binder so you can continue to cover the core (figure 26).

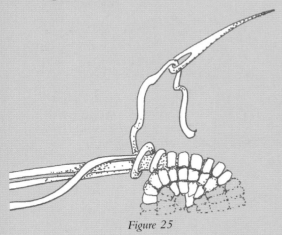

Figure 25

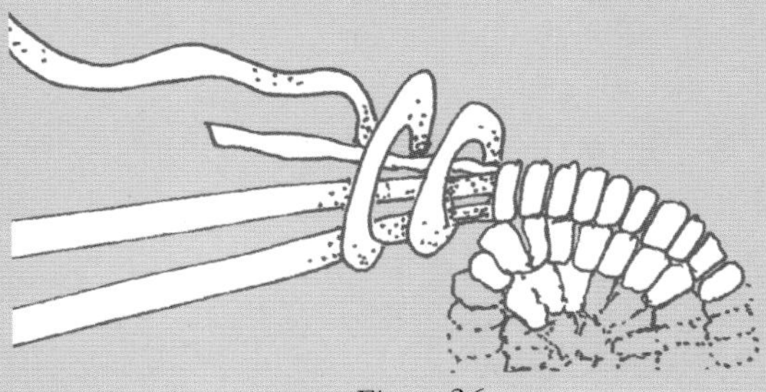

Figure 26

3. To use the tying method, use a double overhand knot to join the tail of the old binder together with the new binder on top of the core (figure 27).

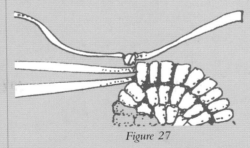

Figure 27

4. Wrap around the tail of the old binder thread to make sure that the end stays at the top of the core and will be covered by the next core you add (figure 28).

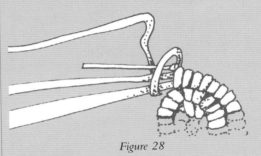

Figure 28

ENDING COILING

The following steps show you how to neatly finish the coiling when you reach the end of your project.

1. Taper the core in preparation for finishing the piece. If you're using linen or wire, cut it at a diagonal. If you're working with pine needles, taper them so that the longest length is closest to the core (figure 29).

2. Continue with the same binding stitch until the core is covered. Bury the end of the binder by stitching back through the core several times so that it is hidden (figure 30).

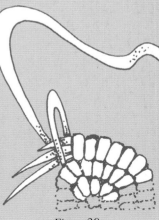

Figure 29

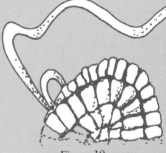

Figure 30

These lightweight earrings are simple to make, and using waxed linen gives you numerous color choices. A light color contrasting with a darker one shows off the pattern created by the lazy stitch.

■ MATERIALS

4-ply black waxed linen, 10 yards (core)

3-ply purple waxed linen, 10 yards of deep purple (binders)

3-ply salmon-colored waxed linen, 10 yards (binders)

Ear wires (findings)

■ TOOLS

Scissors

Tapestry needle

Needle-nose pliers

■ TECHNIQUES

Beginning a flat oval piece (see page 134)

Lazy stitch (see page 136)

Adding binder material (see page 137)

Ending coiling (see page 137)

Finishes (see page 20)

■ INSTRUCTIONS

1. Cut each of the waxed linen lengths in half.

2. Thread a length of the purple linen onto the tapestry needle, and begin to wrap the core of black linen with it. Cover about ³/₄ inch with purple linen (photo 1). Add a few extra wraps to cover a bend in the core, and fold the core to the other side.

Photo 1

2. Connect the second row with lazy stitches followed by two wraps of the core until you close the oval (photo 2).

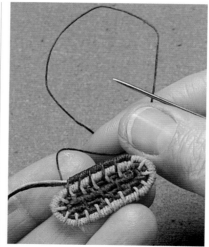

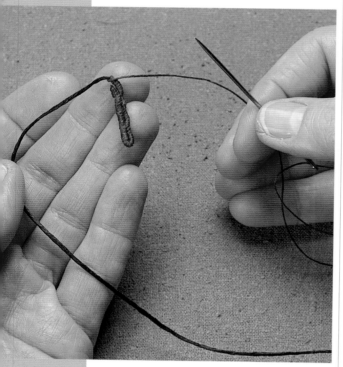

Photo 2

3. Add in the salmon-colored linen, leaving the purple intact, and use the lazy stitch followed by two wraps to complete the third row.

4. Begin the final row by wrapping the core with the salmon color for a small area at one end of the oval shape, or what forms the top of the earring. When done, cut off the salmon thread. Pull out the remaining purple linen from the core, and use it to complete the row of coiling (photo 3).

Photo 3

5. End the coiling as described in the introductory section of this chapter.

6. Create the other matching earring with the same patterning. Use needle-nose pliers to open the connection on each ear wire, and hook each around the last coil. Close the wires with the pliers.

VARIATION

FREE-FORM COILED NECKLACE

THIS PROJECT SHOWS HOW YOU CAN USE COILING TO CREATE FLAT SHAPED PIECES THAT BEGIN WITH A CIRCULAR CENTER. THE FINGERS ARE SIMPLY EXTENSIONS OF THE CORE, BENT INTO CURVED SHAPES.

■ MATERIALS

7-ply black waxed linen, 30 yards (binder)

18-gauge copper wire, 15 yards (core)

7-ply brown waxed linen (neck cord)

Medium-sized stone and glass beads (embellishment)

■ TOOLS

Scissors

Tapestry needle

Wire cutters

Needle-nose pliers

■ INSTRUCTIONS

1. Cut off 10 feet of black waxed linen, and thread one end through a tapestry needle. Cut off 3 feet of wire. Make a round base by wrapping the wire with the linen (photo 1).

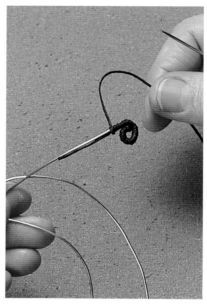

Photo 1

2. To this round piece add three full coils using a lazy stitch with two wraps between each stitch (photo 2).

Photo 2

3. To add the first curved shape (the pinkie finger) to this circular shape, begin by wrapping the wire core approximately 20 times. Use pliers to carefully bend the wire, forming the tip of the finger. About 1/4 inch beneath the tip, use a lazy stitch to connect both sides (photo 3).

Photo 3

4. Keep wrapping the linen on the wire, and when you reach the circle, use a lazy stitch to connect the finger shape to it through the last core (photo 4). Continue adding fingers to emulate a hand. Shape and wrap the thumb last.

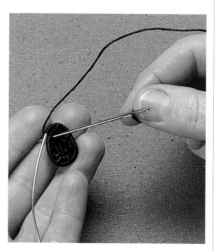

Photo 4

5. Attach the wire (bottom of the thumb) to the outer core by looping the linen through the last core several times. Bend the wire away from the hand to form the hanger for it. Continue wrapping the linen around the wire, covering approximately 1 inch (photo 5).

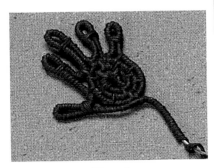

Photo 5

6. Use the tapestry needle to stitch under the last few wraps to secure the end. Cut the thread.

7. Form a hanger for the hand by bending the wire as shown (figure 1).

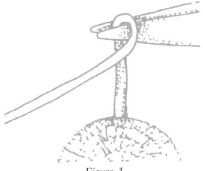

Figure 1

8. Tightly wrap the end of the wire back towards the hand, covering the linen (figure 2). Cut the end of the wire to avoid sharp edges (figure 3).

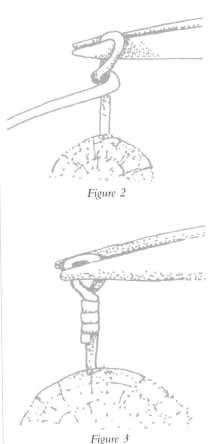

Figure 2

Figure 3

9. Create four more hand pendants using the same process.

10. Make a cord for the necklace from the brown waxed linen. Thread several beads on the cord, placing them about a third of the way down it, and secure them in place with knots on either side. Skip about an inch on the cord, and tie another knot before sliding on more beads, followed by one of the hand pendants.

11. Continue to add beads and pendants. When you're done, add another set of beads to the other side of the necklace.

12. Tie beads onto the ends of each neck cord, and knot the cord at the desired length.

VARIATION

Use traditional pine needle coiling to make this lovely circular piece. It incorporates most of the coiling techniques that you've learned about in this chapter.

■ MATERIALS

Raffia, 15 to 20 lengths, each approximately 5 feet long (binder)

Long pine needles, 50 to 60 (core)

Bar pin back with holes for stitching, 1 inch wide (finding)

■ TOOLS

Tools

Scissors

Tapestry needle

■ TECHNIQUES

Beginning a flat circular piece (see page 132)

Figure-eight stitch (see page 135)

Lazy stitch (see page 136)

Split stitch (see page 136)

Adding binder material (see page 137)

Adding core material (see page 136)

Ending coiling (see page 137)

1. Prepare the pine needles by soaking them in warm water. Reduce the diameter of the raffia by pulling it apart lengthwise.

2. Thread the raffia into the tapestry needle. Begin the flat circular center of the piece by coiling the pine needles and stitching them with the raffia.

3. Hold the center with the longer ends of the core to the left to begin the next rows of stitching. Position the binder raffia thread so that you can stitch around the top of the last core from the back (photo 1).

4. Use a figure-eight stitch to add three to five coils (photo 2). Add in a length of new binder material, when needed, by using a double overhand knot to join the tail of the old binder with the new one on top of the core. As you wrap the core, add in separated pine needles as they run out.

5. Next, use lazy stitches spaced about 1/8 inch apart to complete one row of coiling, providing the setup for the split stitch that follows. Use split stitches spaced about 1/8 inch apart to add about eight more rows of coiling, exposing the pine needle core (photo 3).

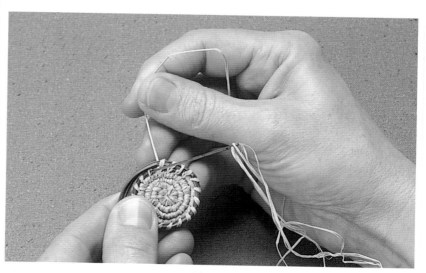

Photo 2

Photo 1

Photo 3

6. To add the decorative border on the final coil, begin by stitching one split stitch on the next row, followed by continuous wrapping until you reach the next split stitch in the design. Add another split stitch, and then wrap again until you reach the next one. Continue this pattern until you complete the last coil.

7. End the coiling.

8. Use raffia to attach the pin back, stitching in and out of the holes. Avoid stitching through to the front of the piece when attaching the pin back (photo 4).

Photo 4

VARIATION

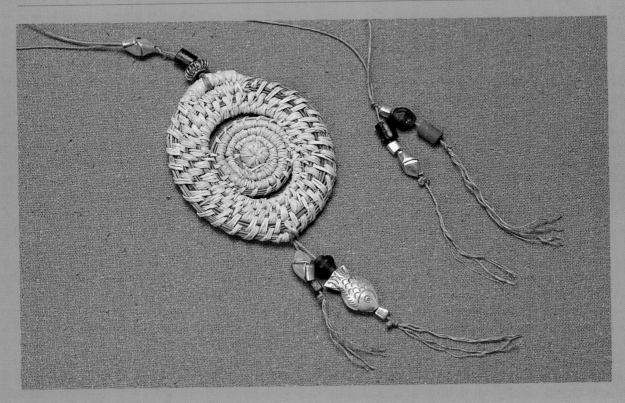

GALLERY

Mary Hettmansperger
Twined Totem Brooch, 2005
3 x ¹/₂ x ¹/₂ inches
2-ply and 3-ply linen; twined
PHOTO BY STEWART O'SHIELDS

Mary Hettmansperger
Medicine Pouch, 2003
2¹/₂ x 2 x ¹/₂ inches
Cedar, birch bark, waxed linen, black
ash, beads; woven
PHOTO BY STEWART O'SHIELDS

Jeanie Pratt
Jade Brooch, 2003
1 x 1¹/₂ x ¹/₈ inches
Sterling silver, 14-karat gold, jade;
hand woven, fabricated
PHOTO BY LINDSAY PRATT

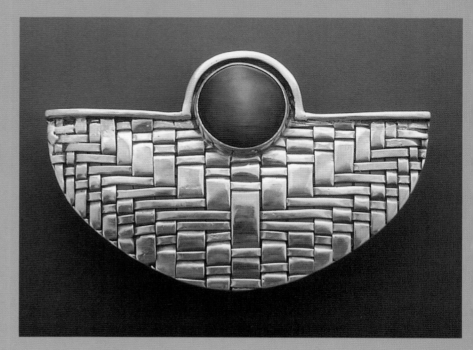

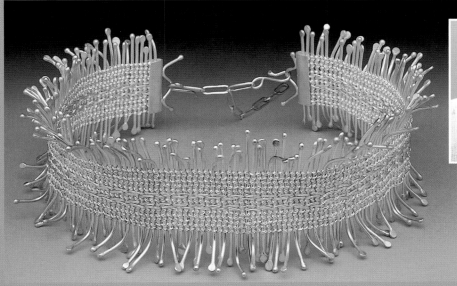

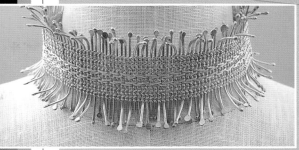

Stephane Threlkeld
Audrey Neckpiece, 2001
2 x 15 x 1¹/₄ inches
Sterling silver, fine silver, 24-karat
kumboo; twined, fabricated
PHOTOS BY GEORGE POST

Jacquelyn Crissman
Savoring Sentiments, 2005
16¹/₂ x 6¹/₂ x 1³/₄ inches
Silver, colored wire, nylon cord, nylon
fibers, garnet, carnelian, amethyst,
feathers, fiber-optic fibers, nickel silver,
magnet, patina; fabricated, twined
PHOTOS BY ERICKA CRISSMAN

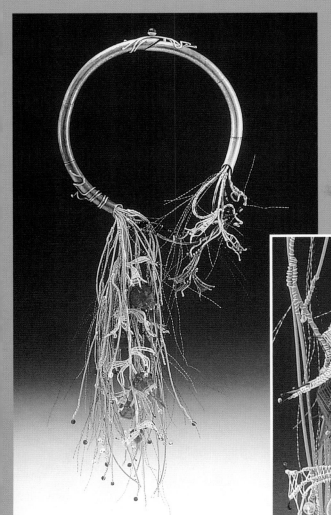

Polly Sutton
Untitled, 2004
1¹/₂ x 1 x ¹/₂ inches
Cedar bark, ash, wire; woven, twined
PHOTO BY BILL WICKETT

Mary Hettmansperger
Cascade, 2005
2 ¹/₂ x ¹/₂ x ¹/₂ inches
Hand-painted waxed linen,
delica beads; twined
PHOTO BY STEWART O'SHIELDS

Dallas Lovett
Pette La Fleur Necklace, 2005
5 x 11 inches
Seed beads, kishi pearls,
silver wire; woven
PHOTO BY TOM FRAZIER

Susan Wood
Woven Sampler
Necklace #4, 1999
1 inch diameter
Sterling silver, fine silver, shakudo, nickel; plaiting, tabby weave, twill weave, mad weave, twining, woven chain
PHOTO BY HAP SAKWA

Jackie Abrams
Woven Pins, 2002
Each, 2 to 2 1/2 inches
Woven of cotton paper, acrylic paint, varnish
PHOTO BY JEFF BAIRD

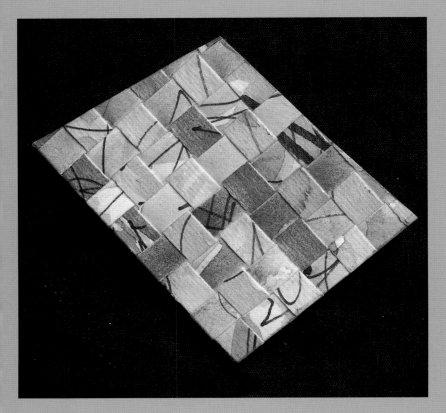

Sue Eyet
Anacin Brooch, 1998
3 x 3 1/2 x 1/2 inches
Vintage tin, wire, recycled telephone wire, black onyx, handmade silver rivets; chase woven
PHOTO BY BOBBY HANSSON

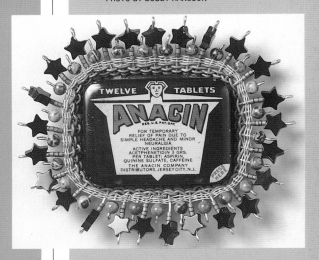

Polly Daeger
Untitled, 2003
10 x 8 x ¹/₄ inch
Copper strips, patina; woven
PHOTO BY LARRY SANDERS

Mary Hettmansperger
Ash Lunch Sack, 2004
3 x ³/₄ x ³/₄ inches
Black ash, waxed linen, beads;
woven
PHOTO BY STEWART O'SHIELDS

Marilyn Moore
Maple Leaf Brooches, 2003
3¹/₂ x 3¹/₄ inches
Polynylon-coated copper wire,
silver-plated wire, copper wire; twined
PHOTO BY ROBERT VINNEDGE

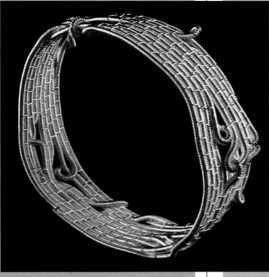

Munya Upin
Garnet Pendant, 1994
1³/₄ x 1³/₄ x ¹/₄ inches
Sterling silver, fine silver, garnet;
woven, fabricated
PHOTO BY ARTIST

Steven Brixner
Coiled Bracelet with Loops,
1978
⁷/₈ x 2³/₄ inches
Sterling silver, fine silver; coiled,
looped, twisted, switchbacks
PHOTO BY ARTIST

Lynne Everett
Hawaii Sunset, 2003
4 x 4 x ¹/₄ inches
Four-ply waxed linen, picture jasper,
beads, charms; knotless netting
PHOTOS BY PEGGY WIEDEMANN

Judy Mulford
Doll Pouch, 1999
4 1/2 x 2 x 1/2 inches
Polymer, waxed linen, fine silver,
beads, pounded tin can lid,
silver charm; looped
PHOTOS BY BILL DEWEY

Anne Miller
Untitled, 2005
1 1/2 x 1 1/2 x 3/16 inches
Paper; painted, woven
PHOTOS BY ORLANDO DAYOAN

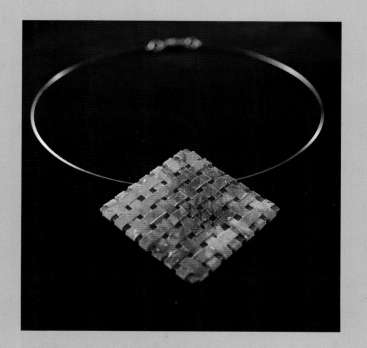

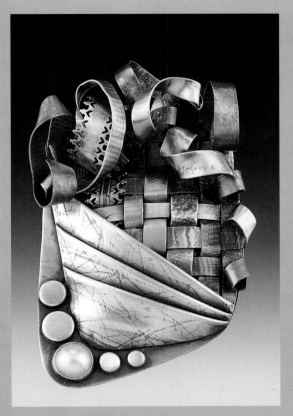

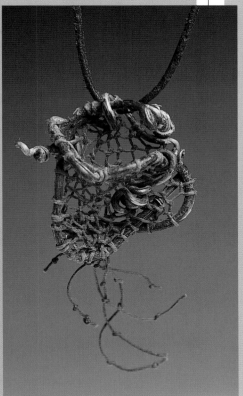

Michele Alexander
Untitled, 2002
2¹/₂ x 1³/₄ inches
Sterling silver, copper, 18-karat gold;
folded, woven, curled, hand fabricated,
soldered
PHOTO BY JERRY ANTHONY

Doris Messick
Tendril Looped Necklace, 2004
2 x 2 x ¹/₂ inches
Waxed linen, grape vine tendrils; looped
PHOTO BY STEWART O'SHIELDS

Mary Hettmansperger
Ice Crystals, 2005
3 x 18 inches
Fuses, beads, split rings; wrapped
PHOTO BY STEWART O'SHIELDS

Patti Hawkins
Twill Baby
2 x 2 x ¼ inches
Dyed and natural black ash; twilled
PHOTO BY STEWART O'SHIELDS

Steven Brixner
Coiled Earrings, **1981**
1½ to 2 inches high
Sterling and fine silver; coiled
PHOTO BY ARTIST

Ed Lee
Choker, **2005**
2½ x 3 x 15 inches
Cotton, paper raffia; knotted, twisted,
stitched, gordian knot
PHOTOS BY JOHN CARLANO

Judy Mulford
Seattle Memory Pouch, 1996
3¹/₂ x 2 x ¹/₂ inches
Waxed linen, amulet, bamboo, charm,
fine silver, beads; looped
PHOTOS BY BILL DEWEY

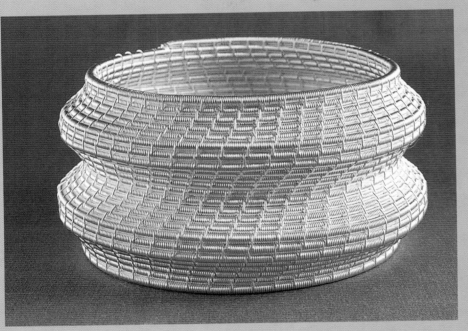

Steven Brixner
Large Coiled Bracelet, 1977
12³/₄ x 3¹/₄ inches
Sterling silver, fine silver;
regular stitching, coiled
PHOTO BY ARTIST

ACKNOWLEDGMENTS

■ Thanks to Lark Books, particularly Carol Taylor, President and Publisher, and Deborah Morgenthal, Vice President and Editor-in-Chief, for the opportunity to produce such a wonderful book.

■ Thanks to Stewart O'Shields for his exquisite photography of the work and the beautifully done process shots. My work has never looked so good! Because of the tremendous creativity and artistic talents of Dana Irwin, who designed the book and styled the photography, each spread is interesting and beautiful.

■ Thanks to the talented artists who contributed images for the gallery and willingly shared their work. And thanks to Rebecca Guthrie, Assistant Editor, for compiling the captions.

■ A very special thank you to the book's editor, Katherine Aimone, whose patience and support delivered this book to its completion. Since this was my first book, the guidance and direction she gave me have been priceless. Not only do I feel I have gained a wonderful book but a new friend.

■ I can't forget my basketry guild friends, AKA Wobies, who have been there for me throughout this process and through all my adventures. I am proud to call all of them my friends.

■ A special thanks to my friends Cass Schorsch, Jackie Abrams, Sandy Whalen, Marilyn Moore, Polly Sutton, Judy Olney, Judy Mulford, Flo Hoppe, Kathy Halter, Nancy Moore Bess, Kathy Jones, and Tammy Johnson, whose encouragement, creative inspiration, lifelong friendship, and endless support have helped me more than they realize.

■ I greatly appreciate Linda Boyle Gibson who assisted with the beginning stages of the technical part of the book. Linda, along with Doris Messick, gave me their support and friendship during the process of writing the book. Thanks gals, I couldn't have done it without both of you.

■ My two best "girls'-night-out" friends, Nancy and Marianne, who made sure I got away from my work to sing, laugh, and reboot my brain. You are both invaluable to my life.

■ Thanks to all my family, with a special thanks to Del, Laura, Martha, and Jean who always support me in my endeavors. You mean the world to me.

■ To my mom, Margaret, whose unwavering love and support throughout my life has been unbelievable. You are truly my hero and role model. Thank you for everything you are and do for me.

■ Thanks to my daughter, Abbey. You are the sunshine of my life. I appreciate your grace, dignity, and patience, especially as I worked on this book while also preparing for your wedding. Congratulations to you and Mac—you are an amazing couple.

■ To my son, Logan, who keeps me young at heart and wears me out…all at the same time. Thanks for taking me out to play even when I thought I should've been working. I love you.

■ And last, but of course not least, thanks to my husband Bob. You are the keeper of my soul and an incredible life partner. You always stop to smell each flower, linger over every kiss, pet each dog, and listen to the birds sing. Thank you so much for patiently taking my hand, slowing me down, and sharing it all with me.

METRIC CONVERSIONS

Inches	Centimeters
1/8	3 mm
1/4	6 mm
3/8	9 mm
1/2	1.3
5/8	1.6
3/4	1.9
7/8	2.2
1	2.5
1 1/4	3.1
1 1/2	3.8
1 3/4	4.4
2	5
2 1/2	6.25
3	7.5
3 1/2	8.8
4	10
4 1/2	11.3
5	12.5
5 1/2	13.8
6	15
7	17.5
8	20
9	22.5
10	25
11	27.5
12	30
1 ft	30
2 ft	60
3 ft	120
4 ft	150
5 ft	180
6 ft	210
7 ft	240
8 ft	270
9 ft	300
10 ft	330

ABOUT THE AUTHOR

Mary Hettmansperger was born in Colorado and now lives in Indiana with her family. She is a fiber artist who has taught basketry for more than 20 years. Her interest in jewelry grew out of the basketmaking process.

She teaches workshops across the country. She has taught at national fiber conferences, including Convergence and Bead and Button, and at institutions such as the John C. Campbell Folk School. During 2005 and 2006, she will be a featured designer on the PBS program titled *Beads Baubles and Jewels*.

In her larger work, she specializes in rib-construction basketry and has exhibited these pieces in many venues, including colleges and commercial galleries. Her innovative basketry has been published in several books and magazines.

DEDICATION

This book is dedicated to the four important men of my life.

My grandpa Ross, who taught me how to live life to the fullest...

My father, Bill, who taught me to love art and whose creative gene still lives through me...

My husband Bob, whose patience, love, and support form a foundation for my life...

And last but not least, my son Logan, whose free spirit has taught me to be a kid again.

INDEX